CAMBRIDGE LIBRARY COLLECTION

Books of enduring scholarly value

Slavery and Abolition

The books reissued in this series include accounts of historical events and movements by eye-witnesses and contemporaries, as well as landmark studies that assembled significant source materials or developed new historiographical methods. The series includes work in social, political and military history on a wide range of periods and regions, giving modern scholars ready access to influential publications of the past.

The Proceedings of the Governor and Assembly of Jamaica, in Regard to the Maroon Negroes

A wealthy planter in the West Indies, Bryan Edwards (1743–1800) lived in Jamaica during the peak of its sugar wealth. Upon his return to England in 1792, he wrote several books on the West Indies, including a multi-volume history of the British colonies. The present work, first published in 1796, relates to the recent conflict between the British and Jamaicans descended from runaway slaves, known as Maroons. Living mostly in isolated mountain communities, the Maroons had been granted certain rights under a 1739 treaty. However, by 1795, with a new governor ruling the island, tensions re-emerged and resulted in another war. Prefaced by Edwards' extended discussion of the Maroons and the origins of the conflict, this collection of documents and letters represents a valuable source in the study of Jamaican history and that of British colonialism in the Caribbean.

Cambridge University Press has long been a pioneer in the reissuing of out-of-print titles from its own backlist, producing digital reprints of books that are still sought after by scholars and students but could not be reprinted economically using traditional technology. The Cambridge Library Collection extends this activity to a wider range of books which are still of importance to researchers and professionals, either for the source material they contain, or as landmarks in the history of their academic discipline.

Drawing from the world-renowned collections in the Cambridge University Library and other partner libraries, and guided by the advice of experts in each subject area, Cambridge University Press is using state-of-the-art scanning machines in its own Printing House to capture the content of each book selected for inclusion. The files are processed to give a consistently clear, crisp image, and the books finished to the high quality standard for which the Press is recognised around the world. The latest print-on-demand technology ensures that the books will remain available indefinitely, and that orders for single or multiple copies can quickly be supplied.

The Cambridge Library Collection brings back to life books of enduring scholarly value (including out-of-copyright works originally issued by other publishers) across a wide range of disciplines in the humanities and social sciences and in science and technology.

The Proceedings of
the Governor
and
Assembly of Jamaica,
in Regard to the
Maroon Negroes

WITH AN INTRODUCTION BY
BRYAN EDWARDS

CAMBRIDGE
UNIVERSITY PRESS

University Printing House, Cambridge, CB2 8BS, United Kingdom

Published in the United States of America by Cambridge University Press, New York

Cambridge University Press is part of the University of Cambridge.

It furthers the University's mission by disseminating knowledge in the pursuit of
education, learning and research at the highest international levels of excellence.

www.cambridge.org
Information on this title: www.cambridge.org/9781108065535

© in this compilation Cambridge University Press 2014

This edition first published 1796
This digitally printed version 2014

ISBN 978-1-108-06553-5 Paperback

THE

PROCEEDINGS

OF THE

Governor and Affembly of Jamaica,

IN REGARD TO THE

MAROON NEGROES:

PUBLISHED BY ORDER OF THE ASSEMBLY.

TO WHICH IS PREFIXED,

Aɴ INTRODUCTORY ACCOUNT,

CONTAINING,

OBSERVATIONS ON THE DISPOSITION, CHARACTER,
MANNERS, AND HABITS OF LIFE,

OF THE MAROONS,

AND

A Detail of the Origin, Progreſs, and Termination

OF

THE LATE WAR BETWEEN THOSE PEOPLE
AND THE WHITE INHABITANTS.

————————

LONDON:
Printed for Jᴏʜɴ Sᴛᴏᴄᴋᴅᴀʟᴇ, Piccadilly.
————
M.DCC.XCVI.

ADVERTISEMENT.

A Copy of the Proceedings of the Governor and Affembly of Jamaica, in the difpofal of the Maroons (printed in that ifland by authority) having found its way to the prefs in London, I was prevailed on to promife an introductory difcourfe to be prefixed to the prefent edition, containing fome account of the Maroon War; with fuch obfervations as occurred to me, during a long acquaintance with thofe people, concerning their fituation, character, and manners. This account is now prefented to the reader. It was written, and partly printed, previous to the late unexpected difcuffion in the Houfe of Commons *. My principal inducement in compiling it was the

* 21ft October.

gratification

gratification of the publick curiofity; but I have now a much ftronger motive for haftening its publication. The good Faith and Honour, the Humanity and Juftice, of the Government of Jamaica, in the conduct of this affair, have been queftioned by high authority *, before the Parliament of Great Britain. It is prefumed that the following fheets will enable the reader to form a correct judgment on the whole proceedings. I am not confcious of having fupprefled a fingle circumftance neceffary to be known, or afferted any one fact which I do not believe to be true.

B. EDWARDS.

London,
7th *November* 1796.

* Mr. Fox.

INTRODUCTION.

SECTION I.

JAMAICA, as every one knows, was con-
quered from the Spaniards, during the
protectorate of Cromwell, in the year 1655,
by an armament under the command of Ad-
miral Penn and General Venables. The Spanish inhabitants are said to have possessed,
before the attack, about 1,500 enslaved
Africans, most of whom, on the surrender of
their masters, retreated to the mountains, from
whence they made frequent excursions to
harass the English. Major-general Sedge-
wick, one of the British officers, in a letter
to Secretary Thurloe (1656) predicts, that
these blacks would prove a thorn in the sides
of the English. He adds, that they gave no
quarter to his men, but destroyed them
whenever they found opportunity; scarce a
week passing without their murdering one or
more of them; and as the soldiers became
more confident and careless, the negroes grew
more enterprising and bloody-minded. "Hav-
" ing no moral sense," continues he, " and
" not understanding what the laws and cus-

a   " toms

" toms of civil nations mean, we know not
" how to capitulate or treat with any of them.
" But be aſſured, they muſt either be deſtroy-
" ed, or brought in, upon ſome terms or
" other; or elſe they will prove a great diſ-
" couragement to the ſettling the country."
What he foretold ſoon came to paſs. At the
latter part of the ſame year (1656) the army
gained ſome trifling ſuccefs againſt them; but
this was immediately afterwards ſeverely re-
taliated by the ſlaughter of forty ſoldiers, cut
off as they were carelefsly rambling from
their quarters. A detachment was immediately
ſent in purſuit of the enemy, which came
up with and killed ſeven or eight of them;
but they ſtill found means means to hold
out, until being hard preſſed the year following by Colonel D'Oyley, who, by his
final overthrow of the Spaniards, had taken
from them all hope of future ſuccour from
their ancient maſters, they became very much
ſtreightened for want of proviſions and ammunition. The main body, under the command of a negro named *Juan de Bolas* (whoſe
place of retreat in the pariſh of Clarendon ſtill
retains his name) at length ſolicited for peace,
and ſurrendered to the Engliſh on terms of

7   pardon

pardon and freedom. A large party, however, (who had now acquired the name of Maroons *) remained in their retreats within the mountains; where they not only augmented their numbers by natural increaſe, but, after the iſland became thicker ſown with plantations, they were frequently reinforced by fugitive ſlaves. At length they grew confident enough of their force to undertake deſcents upon the interior planters, many of whom they murdered, from time to time, without the leaſt provocation; and by their barbarities and outrages intimidated the whites from venturing to any confiderable diſtance from the ſea coaſt.

In 1663 the Lieutenant-governor, Sir Charles Lyttelton, and his council, iſſued a

* The word ſignifies, among the Spaniſh Americans, according to Mr. Long, *Hog-hunters:* the woods abounding with the wild boar, and the purſuit of them conſtituting the chief employment of fugitive negroes. *Marráno* is the Spaniſh word for a young pig. The following is the derivation, however, given in the Encyclopédie, article *Maron :* "On appelle *marons*, dans les iſles Françoiſes les nègres fugitifs. Ce terme vient du mot Eſpagnol *Simaran* qui ſignifie un Singe. Les Eſpagnols crurent ne devoir pas faire plus d'honneur à leurs malheureux eſclaves fugitifs, que de les appeller *ſinges*, parcequ'ils ſe retiroient comme ces animaux aux fonds des bois et n'en ſortoient que pour cueillir des fruits qui ſe trouvoient dans les lieux les plus voiſins de leur retrait."

proclamation,

proclamation, offering a full pardon, twenty acres of land, and freedom from all manner of flavery, to each of them who fhould furrender. But I do not find that any of them were inclined to accept the terms offered, or quit their favage way of life. On the contrary, they were better pleafed with the more ample range they poffeffed in the woods, where their hunting grounds were not yet encroached upon by fettlements. They took effectual care, indeed, that no fettlement fhould be eftablifhed near them; for they butchered every white family that ventured to feat itfelf any confiderable diftance inland. When the Governor perceived that the proclamation wrought no effect, Juan de Bolas, who was now made Colonel of the Black Regiment, was fent to endeavour their reduction; but in the profecution of this fervice he fell into an ambufcade, and was cut to pieces. In March, 1664, Captain Colbeck, of the white militia, was employed for the fame purpofe. He went by fea to the north fide; and, having gained fome advantages over the Maroons, he returned with one who pretended to treat for the reft. This embaffy, however, was only calculated to amufe the whites, and gain fome refpite, for

the

the Maroons no fooner found themfelves in a condition to act, and the white inhabitants lulled into fecurity, than they began to renew hoftilities, murdering, as before, every white perfon, without diftinction of fex or age, who came within their reach.

In this way they continued to diftrefs the ifland for upward of forty years, during which time forty-four acts of Affembly were paffed, and at leaft £.240,000 expended for their fuppreffion. In 1730 they were grown fo formidable, under a very able general, named Cudjoe, that it was found expedient to ftrengthen the colony againft them by two regiments of regular troops, which were afterwards formed into independent companies, and employed, with other hired parties, and the whole body of militia, in their reduction. In the year 1734 Captain Stoddart, who commanded one of thefe parties, projected and executed with great fuccefs, an attack of the Maroon windward town, called Nauny, fituate on one of the higheft mountains in the ifland. Having provided fome portable fwivel guns, he filently approached, and reached within a fmall diftance of their quarters undifcovered. After

halting,

halting, for fome time, he began to afcend by the only path leading to their town. He found it fleep, rocky, and difficult, and not wide enough to admit the paffage of two perfons abreaft. However, he furmounted thefe obftacles; and having gained a fmall eminence, commanding the huts in which the negroes were afleep, he fixed his little train of artillery to the beft advantage, and fired upon them fo brifkly, that many were flain in their habitations, and feveral more threw themfelves headlong down precipices. Captain Stoddart purfued the advantage, killed numbers, took many prifoners, and in fhort fo completely de-ftroyed, or routed the whole body, that they were unable afterwards to effect any enterprize of moment in this quarter of the ifland.

About the fame time another party of the blacks, having perceived that a body of the militia ftationed at the barrack of Bagnel's thicket, in St. Mary's parifh, under the com-mand of Colonel Charlton, ftrayed heedlefsly from their quarters, and kept no order, formed a project to cut them off, and whilft the officers were at dinner, attended by a very few of their men, the Maroons rufhed fud-

denly

denly from the adjacent woods and attacked them. Several pieces were difcharged, the report of which alarmed the militia, who imdiately ran to their arms, and came up in time to refcue their officers from deftruction. The Maroons were repulfed, and forced to take fhelter in the woods, but the militia did not think fit to purfue them. Some rumours of this fkirmifh reached Spanifh Town, which is diftant from the fpot about thirty miles; and, as all the circumftances were not known, the inhabitants were thrown into the moft dreadful alarm, from apprehenfions that the Maroons had defeated Charlton, and were in full march to attack the town. Afcough, then commander in chief, participating in the general panick, ordered the trumpets to found, the drums to beat, and in a few hours collected a body of horfe and foot, who went to meet the enemy. On the fecond day after their departure they came to a place where, by the fires which remained unextinguifhed, they fuppofed the Maroons had lodged the preceding night. They therefore followed the track, and foon after got fight of them. Captain Edmunds, who commanded the detachment, difpofed his men for action; but the

Maroons

Maroons declined engaging, and fled different ways. Several of them, however, were slain in the pursuit, and others made prisoners. These two victories reduced their strength, and filled them with so much terror that they never afterwards appeared in any considerable body, nor dared to make any stand; indeed, from the commencement of the war till this period, they had not once ventured a pitched battle, but skulked about the skirts of remote plantations, surprising stragglers, and murdering the whites by two or three at a time, or when they were too few to make any resistance. By night, they seized the favourable opportunity that darkness gave them, of stealing into the settlements, where they set fire to cane fields and out-houses, killed all the cattle they could find, and carried the slaves into captivity. By this dastardly method of conducting the war, they did infinite mischief to the whites, without much exposing their own persons to danger, for they always cautiously avoided fighting, except with a number so disproportionally inferior to themselves as to afford them a pretty sure expectation of victory. They knew every secret avenue of the country; so that they could

either

either conceal themſelves from purſuit, or ſhift their ravages from place to place, as circumſtances required. Such were the many diſadvantages under which the Engliſh had to deal with thoſe deſultory foes; who were not reducible by any regular plan of attack; who poſſeſſed no plunder to allure or reward the aſſailants; nor had any thing to loſe, except life, and a wild and ſavage freedom.

Previous to the ſucceſſes above mentioned, the diſtreſs into which the planters were thrown, may be collected from the ſenſe which the legiſlature of Jamaica expreſſed in ſome of their acts. In the year 1733, they ſet forth, " that the Maroons had, within a few years, greatly increaſed, notwithſtanding all the meaſures that had then been concerted, and made uſe of, for their ſuppreſſion; in particular, that they had grown very formidable in the North Eaſt, North Weſt, and South Weſtern diſtricts of the iſland, to the great terror of his Majeſty's ſubjects in thoſe parts, who had greatly ſuffered by the frequent robberies, murders, and depredations committed by them; that in the pariſhes of Clarendon, St. Ann, St. Elizabeth, Weſtmorland, Hanover,

and

and St. James's, they were confiderably mul-
tiplied, and had large fettlements among the
mountains, and leaft acceffible parts ; whence
they plundered all around them, and caufed
feveral plantations to be thrown up and aban-
doned, and prevented many valuable tracts of
land from being cultivated, to the great prejudice and diminution of his Majefty's reve-
nue, as well as of the trade, navigation, and
confumption of Britifh manufactures ; and to
the manifeft weakening, and preventing further increafe of ftrength and inhabitants, in
the ifland." We may learn from hence, what
extenfive mifchief may be perpetrated by the
moft defpicable and cowardly enemy. The
Affembly, perceiving that the employment of
flying parties had proved ineffectual, by the
length of their marches, the difficulty of fubfifting them in the woods for fo long a time as
the fervice required, and the facility with
which the Maroons eluded their purfuit, ordered feveral defenfible houfes, or barracks,
fortified with baftions, to be erected in different parts, as near as poffible to the enemy's
moft favourite haunts : in every one of thefe
they placed a ftrong garrifon, who were regu-
larly

larly fubfifted, and roads of communication were opened from one to the other. Thefe garrifons were compofed of white and black fhot and baggage negroes, who were all duly trained. Every captain was allowed a pay of ten pounds, the lieutenants each five pounds, ferjeants four pounds, and privates two pounds per month. They were fubjected to rules and articles of war; and the whole body put under the Governor's immediate order, to be employed, conjunctly or feparately, as he fhould fee occafion. Their general plan of duty, as directed by the law, was to make excurfions from the barracks, fcower the woods and mountains, and deftroy the provifion gardens and haunts of the Maroons; and that they might not return without effecting fome fervice, they were required to take twenty days provifion with them on every fuch expedition. Every barrack, befides, *was furnifhed with a pack of dogs, provided by the churchwardens of the refpective parifhes*; it being forefeen that thefe animals would prove extremely ferviceable, not only in guarding *againft furprizes in the night,* but in tracking the enemy.

This

This arrangement was the moſt judicious hitherto contrived for their effectual reduction; for ſo many fortreſſes, ſtationed in the very centre of their uſual retreats, well ſupplied with every neceſſary, gave the Maroons a conſtant and vigorous annoyance, and in ſhort became the chief means of bringing on that treaty which afterwards put an end to this tireſome war.

About the year 1737, the Aſſembly reſolved on taking two hundred of the Moſquito Indians into their pay, to haſten the ſuppreſſion of the Maroons. They paſſed an act for rendering free Negroes, Mulattoes, and Indians more uſeful, and forming them into companies, with proper encouragements. Some ſloops were diſpatched to the Moſquito ſhore; and that number of Indians was brought into the iſland, formed into companies under their own officers, and allowed forty ſhillings a month for pay, beſides ſhoes and other articles. White guides were aſſigned to conduct them to the enemy, and they gave proofs of great ſagacity in this ſervice. It was their practice to obſerve the moſt

profound

profound filence in marching to the enemy's quarters; and when they had once hit upon a track, they were fure to difcover the haunt to which it led. They effected confiderable fervice, and were, indeed, the moft proper troops to be employed in that fpecies of action, which is known in America by the name of *bufh-fighting*. They were well rewarded for their good conduct, and afterwards dif-miffed to their own country, when the pacification took place with the Maroons.

In 1738, Governor Trelawney, by the advice of the principal gentlemen of the ifland, propofed overtures of peace with the Maroon chiefs. Both parties were now grown heartily wearied out with this tedious conflict. The white inhabitants wifhed relief from the horrors of continual alarms, the hardfhip of military duty, and the intolerable burthen of maintaining the army. The Maroons were not lefs anxious for an accommodation: they were hemmed in, and clofely befet on all fides; their provifions deftroyed, and themfelves reduced to fo miferable a condition, by famine and inceffant attacks, that

Cudjoe

Cudjoe afterwards declared, that if peace had not been offered to them, they had no choice left but either to be ftarved, lay violent hands on themfelves, or furrender to the Englifh at difcretion. The extremity of their cafe, however, was not at that time known to the white inhabitants, and their number was fuppofed to be twice as great as it was afterwards found to be. The articles of pacification (which I have fubjoined) were therefore ratified with the Maroon chiefs, and fifteen hundred acres of land affigned to one body of them *, and one thoufand acres to another, which the legiflature fecured to them and their pofterity in perpetuity. The Affembly, by fubfequent laws, augmented the premium allowed the Maroons for apprehending fugitive flaves, to three pounds per head ; and they paffed many other

* This was the body that fettled in Trelawney Town, and are the anceftors of thofe who have lately taken up arms. The other Maroon negroes were thofe of Acompong Town, Crawford Town, and Nauny Town, to each of which lands were allotted. The aggregate number, in 1795, was about 1600, men, women, and children.

regulations

regulations for their better government and protection, for preventing their purchafing and harbouring negro flaves, and for directing in what manner they fhould be tried in the cafe of fe-lony, and other crimes, committed againft the whites †, and thus an end was at length hap-

pily

† On complaint made, on oath, to a juftice of peace, of any felony, burglary, robbery, or other offence whatfoever, having been committed by Maroon negroes, he is required to grant a warrant to apprehend the offenders, and to have all perfons brought before him, or fome other juftice, that can give evidence; and if, upon examination, it appears that there are grounds for publick trial, the juftice is to commit the accufed unlefs the offence be bailable, and bind over the witneffes. They are to be tried where the quarter feffions are held, or where parochial bufinefs is ufually tranfacted, in the fol-lowing manner :—The juftice is to call in two other juftices (who muft attend, or forfeit twenty pounds each), and they are to fummon fifteen perfons, fuch as are ufually impanelled to ferve on juries, to appear at a fpecified time, who forfeit five pounds each if they neglect. There muft be ten days between the complaint and the trial. Of the fifteen per-fons fummoned, the firft twelve who appear are to compofe a jury. If the Maroon be found guilty, the juftices may give fentence, according to law, of death, tranfportation, public whipping, or confinement to hard labour for not more than twelve months. Execution of women with child is to be refpited until a reafonable time after delivery;

and

pily put to this tedious and ruinous conteft; a
conteft which, while it lafted, feemed to
portend nothing lefs than the ruin of the
whole colony.

*Articles of pacification with the Maroons of
Trelawney Town, concluded March the
firft, 1738.*

In the name of God, Amen, Whereas
Captain Cudjoe, Captain Acompong, Captain Johnny, Captain Cuffee, Captain Quaco,
and feveral other Negroes, their dependents
and adherents, have been in a ftate of war
and hoftility, for feveral years paft, againft
our fovereign lord the King, and the inhabitants of this ifland; and whereas peace
and friendfhip among mankind, and the
preventing the effufion of blood, is agreeable

and where fentence of death or tranfportation fhall be paffed
(except for rebellious confpiracies,) execution is to be refpited until the Governor's pleafure be fignified; the juftices
may alfo refpite the execution of any other fentence till his
pleafure be known, if they fee caufe. Where feveral are
capitally convicted for the fame offence, one only is to fuffer
death, except for murder or rebellion.

to

to God, confonant to reafon, and defired by
every good man; and whereas his Majefty
George the Second, King of Great Britain,
France, and Ireland, and of Jamaica Lord,
Defender of the Faith, &c. has by his letters
patent, dated February the twenty-fourth, one
thoufand feven hundred and thirty-eight, in
the twelfth year of his reign, granted full power
and authority to John Guthrie and Francis Sad-
ler, Efquires, to negotiate and finally conclude
a treaty of peace and friendfhip with the afore-
faid Captain Cudjoe, and the reft of his captains,
adherents, and others his men; they mutually,
fincerely, and amicably, have agreed to the
following articles: Firft, That all hoftilities
fhall ceafe on both fides for ever. Secondly,
That the faid Captain Cudjoe, the reft of his
captains, adherents, and men, fhall be for
ever hereafter in a perfect ftate of freedom
and liberty, excepting thofe who have been
taken by them, or fled to them, within two
years laft paft, if fuch are willing to return
to their faid mafters and owners, with full
pardon and indemnity from their faid mafters
or owners for what is paft; provided always,

that,

that, if they are not willing to return, they
shall remain in subjection to Captain Cudjoe
and in friendship with us, according to the
form and tenor of this treaty. Thirdly, That
they shall enjoy and possess, for themselves
and posterity for ever, all the lands situate
and lying between Trelawney Town and the
Cockpits, to the amount of fifteen hundred
acres, bearing northwest from the said Trelawney Town. Fourthly, That they shall
have liberty to plant the said lands with coffee, cocoa, ginger, tobacco, and cotton, and
to breed cattle, hogs, goats, or any other
stock, and dispose of the produce or in-
crease of the said commodities to the inhabitants of this island; provided always, that
when they bring the said commodities to
market, they shall apply first to the custos, or
any other magistrate of the respective parishes
where they expose their goods to sale, for a
licence to vend the same. Fifthly, That
Captain Cudjoe, and all the Captain's adherents, and people now in subjection to him,
shall all live together within the bounds of
Trelawney Town, and that they have liberty

to

to hunt where they ſhall think fit, except
within three miles of any ſettlement, crawl,
or pen; provided always, that in caſe the
hunters of Captain Cudjoe and thoſe of other
ſettlements meet, then the hogs to be equally
divided between both parties. Sixthly, That the
ſaid Captain Cudjoe, and his ſucceſſors, do uſe
their beſt endeavours to take, kill, ſupprefs, or
deſtroy, either by themſelves, or jointly with
any other number of men, commanded on that
ſervice by his excellency the Governor, or
Commander in Chief for the time being, all
rebels whereſoever they be, throughout this
iſland, unleſs they ſubmit to the ſame terms
of accommodation granted to Captain Cudjoe,
and his ſucceſſors. Seventhly, That in caſe
this iſland be invaded by any foreign enemy,
the ſaid Captain Cudjoe, and his ſucceſſors
hereinafter named or to be appointed, ſhall
then, upon notice given, immediately repair
to any place the Governor for the time being ſhall appoint, in order to repel the ſaid
invaders with his or their utmoſt force, and to
ſubmit to the orders of the Commander in
Chief on that occaſion. Eighthly, That if
any white man ſhall do any manner of injury

to

to Captain Cudjoe, his fucceffors, or any of his
or their people, they fhall apply to any commanding officer or magiftrate in the neighbourhood for juftice; *and in cafe Captain
Cudjoe, or any of his people, fhall do any injury
to any white perfon, he fhall fubmit himfelf, or
deliver up fuch offenders to juftice.* Ninthly,
That if any negroes fhall hereafter run away
from their mafters or owners, and fall into
Captain Cudjoe's hands, they fhall immediately be fent back to the chief magiftrate
of the next parifh where they are taken; and
thofe that bring them are to be fatisfied for
their trouble, as the legiflature fhall appoint *
Tenthly, That all negroes taken, fince the
raifing of this party by Captain Cudjoe's
people, fhall immediately be returned. Ele-
venthly, That Captain Cudjoe, and his fucceffors, fhall wait on his Excellency, or the Commander in Chief for the time being, every
year, if thereunto required. Twelfth, That
Captain Cudjoe, during his life, and the cap-

* The Affembly granted a premium of thirty fhillings
for each fugitive flave returned to his owner by the Maroons, befides expences.

tains

tains fucceeding him, fhall have full power to inflict any punifhment they think proper for crimes committed by their men among themfelves, death only excepted; in which cafe, if the Captain thinks they deferve death, he fhall be obliged to bring them before any juftice of the peace, who fhall order proceedings on their trial equal to thofe of other free negroes. Thirteenth, That Captain Cudjoe, with his people, fhall cut, clear, and keep open, large and convenient roads from Trelawney Town to Weftmorland and St. James's, and if poffible to St. Elizabeth's. Fourteenth, That two white men, to be nominated by his Excellency, or the Commander in Chief for the time being, fhall conftantly live and refide with Captain Cudjoe and his fucceffors, in order to maintain a friendly correfpondence with the inhabitants of this ifland. Fifteenth, That Captain Cudjoe fhall, during his life, be Chief Commander in Trelawney Town; after his deceafe the command to devolve on his brother Captain Accompong; and in cafe of his deceafe, on his next brother Captain Johnny; and, failing him, Captain Cuffee fhall fucceed; who is to be fucceeded by Captain Quaco;

and

and after all their demifes, the Governor, or Commander in Chief for the time being, fhall appoint, from time to time, whom he thinks fit for that command.

In teftimony, &c. &c.

SEC.

SECTION II.

THE preceding Section confifts chiefly of
an extract from the Hiftory of Jamaica,
by EDWARD LONG, Efq. publifhed in 1774,
whofe account I have chofen to adopt, rather
than offer a narrative of my own; for two reafons, firft, becaufe I have nothing to add, concerning the origin of the Maroons, to what
Mr. Long has fo diftinctly related; and, fe-
condly, becaufe its adoption exempts me
from all fufpicion of having fabricated a
tale, calculated to juftify certain circumftances and tranfactions, of which complaint
was made in the Britifh Parliament *, and
to which due attention fhall hereafter be
paid. In the meanwhile I fhall take up and
continue the fubject where Mr. Long left it,
beginning with fome reflections on the fituation, character, manners, and habits of life of
the Maroon negroes; and thus tracing the
caufe of their late revolt to its origin.

* March 1796.

The

The claufe in the treaty, by which thefe
people were compelled to refide within certain boundaries in the interior country, apart
from all other negroes, was founded, probably,
on the apprehenfion that, by fuffering them
to intermix with the negroes in flavery, the
example which they would thereby continually prefent of fuccefsful hoftility, might
prove contagious, and create in the minds of
the flaves an impatience of fubordination, and
a difpofition for revolt : but time has abun-
dantly proved that it was an ill-judged and a
fatal regulation. The Maroons, inftead of being
eftablifhed into feparate hordes or communities, in the ftrongeft parts of the interior country, fhould have been encouraged by all poffible means to frequent the towns and to intermix with the negroes at large. All diftinction between the Maroons and the other free
blacks would foon have been ioft ; the greater
number would have prevailed over the lefs :
whereas the policy of keeping them a diftinct
people, continually inured to arms, intro-
duced among them what the French call an
efprit de corps, or a community of fentiments
and

and interefts : and concealing from them the
powers and refources of the whites, taught
them to feel, and at the fame time highly to
overvalue, their own relative ftrength and importance.

It has been urged againft the colonial legiflature, as another, and a ftill greater, overfight,
that after the conclufion of the treaty, no
manner of attention was given to the im-
provement of thefe ignorant people in civilization and morals! The office of *fuperintendant*, it has been faid, and I believe truly,
was commonly beftowed on perfons of no
education or confequence, and foon became a
mere *finecure*. Mr. Long obferved, many
years ago, that the Maroons would probably
prove more faithful allies, and better fubjects,
if pains were taken to inftil into their minds a
few notions of honefty and religion ; and the
eftablifhment of fchools, and the erection of
a chapel in each of the towns, were recommended, as meafures of indifpenfible neceffity.

That thefe obfervations are altogether ill
founded, I will not prefume to affirm. Man,
in his favage ftate, in all parts of the world,

is

is the flave of fuperftition ; and it is the duty
and policy of a good government (let its fyftem of religion be what it may) to direct the
weakneffes of our fellow creatures to the pro-
motion of their happinefs. The Chriftian is
not only the beft fyftem of religion calculated
for the attainment of that end, but, by leading
the mind to the knowledge of truth and im-
mortality, contributes more than any other to
amend the heart, and exalt the human character. It is a fyftem of humility, meeknefs,
and loving kindnefs : and although we fhould
admit, with the eloquent hiftorian of the Ro-
man Empire *, that " the fuperftitions of
Paganifm always bore the appearance of pleafure, and often of virtue ;" we muft, at the
fame time, allow that they afforded no con-
folation to the wretched ; they furnifhed but
few leffons of juftice, and none of forgive-
nefs and mercy !

Of thefe high and important truths I hope
that I am fully fenfible. Yet I cannot fup-
prefs the opinion which I have long fince en-
tertained, that the converfion of favage men
from a life of barbarity to the knowledge and

* Gibbon.

practice

practice of Chriftianity, is a work of much greater difficulty than many pious and excellent perfons in Great Britain feem fondly to imagine.

Concerning the Maroons, they are in general ignorant of our language, and all of them attached to the gloomy fuperftitions of Africa (derived from their anceftors) with fuch enthufiaftick zeal and reverential ardour, as I think can only be eradicated with their lives. The Gentoos of India are not, I conceive, more fincere in their faith, than the negroes of Guinea in believing the prevalence of *Obi*, and the fupernatural power of their *Obeah* men. Obftacles like thefe, accompanied with the fierce and fordid manners which I fhall prefently defcribe, few clergymen would, I think, be pleafed to encounter, left they might experience all the fufferings, without acquiring the glory of martyrdom.

Under difadvantages of fuch magnitude was founded the firft legal eftablifhment of our Maroon allies in Jamaica. Inured, for a long feries of years, to a life of warfare within the ifland, it is a matter of aftonifhment that they fubmitted, for any length of time, to any fyftem of fubordination or government whatever. It is

probable

probable they were chiefly induced to remain
quiet by the great encouragement that was
held out to them for the apprehending fugitive flaves, and being allowed to range over
the uncultivated country without interruption,
pofleffing an immenfe wildernefs for their
hunting grounds. Thefe purfuits, by giving
full employment to the reftlefs and turbulent
among them, diverted them from fchemes of
greater enterprize and projects of mifchief.
Their game was the wild boar, which abounds
in the interior parts of Jamaica; and the Ma--
roons had a method of curing the flefh without falting it. This commodity they frequently brought to market in the towns; and,
with the money arifing from the fale, and the
rewards which they received for the delivery
to their owners of runaway flaves, they pur-
chafed falted beef, fpirituous liquors, tobacco,
fire-arms, and ammunition, fetting little or
no account on clothing of any kind, and
regarding as fuperfluous and ufelefs, moft of
thofe things which every people, in the loweft
degree of civilization, would confider as almoft abfolutely neceffary to human exiftence.

Their

Their language was a barbarous diffonance of the African dialects, with a mixture of Spanifh and broken Englifh; and their thoughts and attention feemed wholly engroffed by their prefent purfuits, and the objects immediately around them, without any reflections on the paft, or folicitude for the future. In common with all the nations of Africa, they believed, however, as I have obferved, in the prevalence of *Obi* (a fort of witchcraft of moft extenfive influence) and the authority which fuch of their old men as had the reputation of wizards, or *Obeah-men*, poffeffed over them, was fometimes very fuccefsfully employed in keeping them in fubordination to their chiefs.

Having, in the refources that have been mentioned, the means of procuring food for their daily fupport, they had no inclination for the purfuits of fober induftry. Their repugnance to the labour of tilling the earth was remarkable. In fome of their villages I never could perceive any veftige of culture; but the fituation of their towns, in fuch cafes, was generally in the neighbourhood of plantations belonging to the whites, from the

provifion

provifion-grounds of which they either pur-
chafed, or ftole, yams, plantains, corn, and
other efculents. When they had no fupply
of this kind, I have fometimes obferved fmall
patches of Indian corn and yams, and perhaps a few ftraggling plaintain trees, near
their habitations ; but the ground was always
in a fhocking ftate of neglect and ruin.

The labours of the field, however, fuch
as they were (as well as every other fpecies of
drudgery) were performed by the women, who
had no other means of clearing the ground
of the vaft and heavy woods with which it
is every where incumbered, than by placing
fire round the trunks of the trees, till they
were confumed in the middle, and fell by
their own weight. It was a fervice of danger; but the Maroons, like all other favage
nations, regarded their wives as fo many
beafts of burthen ; and felt no more concern
at the lofs of one of them, than a white
planter would have felt at the lofs of a bul-
lock. Polygamy too, with their other African
cuftoms, prevailed among the Maroons univerfally. Some of their principal men claim-
ed from two to fix wives, and the miferies of
their

their fituation left thefe poor creatures neither
leifure nor inclination to quarrel with each
other.

This fpirit of brutality, which the Marcons
always difplayed towards their wives, extended in fome degree to their children. The
parental authority was at all times moft
harfhly exerted ; but more efpecially towards
the females. I have been affured that it was
not an uncommon circumftance for a father,
in a fit of rage or drunkennefs, to feize
his own infant, which had offended him by
crying, and dafh it againft a rock, with a degree of violence which often proved fatal.
This he did without any apprehenfion of punifhment; for the fuperintendant, on fuch occafions, generally found it prudent to keep his
diftance, or be filent. Nothing can more
ftrikingly demonftrate the forlorn and abject
condition of the young women among the
Maroons, than the circumftance which every
gentleman, who has vifited them on feftive
occafions, or for the gratification of curiofity,
knows to be true ; the offering their own
daughters, by the firft men among them,
to their vifitors ; and bringing the poor girls
                                    forward,

forward, with or without their confent, for the purpofe of proftiaution.

Vifits of this kind (though I believe not frequent) were indeed but too acceptable both to the Maroons and their daughters; for they generally ended in drunkennefs and riot. The vifitors too were not only fleeced of their money, but were likewife obliged *to furnifh the feaft*, it being indifpenfibly neceffary, on fuch occafions, to fend beforehand wine and provifions of all kinds; and if the guefts expected to fleep on beds and in linen, like gentlemen, they muft provide thofe articles alfo for themfelves. The Maroons, however, if the party confifted of perfons of confequence, would confider themfelves as highly honoured, and would fupply wild boar, land-crabs, pigeons, and fifh, and entertain their guefts with a hearty and boifterous kind of hofpitality, which had at leaft the charms of novelty and fingularity to recommend it.

On fuch occafions, a mock fight always conftituted a part of the entertainment. Mr. Long has given the following defcription of a fcene of this kind, which was exhibited by the Trelawney-Town Maroons, in the prefence

of

of the Governor, in 1764. "No fooner (he obferves) did the horn found the fignal, than they all joined in a moft hideous yell, or war-hoop, and bounded into action. With amazing agility they ran, or rather rolled, through their various firings and evolutions. This part of their exercife, indeed, more juftly deferves to be ftiled *evolution* than any that is practifed by the regular troops; for they fire ftooping almoft to the very ground; and no fooner is the piece difcharged, than they throw themfelves into a thoufand antick geftures, and tumble over and over, fo as to be continually fhifting their place; the intention of which is to elude the fhot, as well as to deceive the aim of their adverfaries, which their nimble and almoft inftantaneous change of pofition renders extremely uncertain. When this part of their exercife was over, they drew their fwords; and winding their horn again, began, in wild and warlike geftures, to advance towards his Excellency, endeavouring to throw as much favage fury into their looks as poffible. On approaching near him, fome waved their rufty blades over his head, then gently laid them

upon

upon it; whilſt others claſhed their arms together in horrid concert. They next brought
their muſkets, and piled them up in heaps at
his feet, &c. &c."

With all this ſeeming fury and affected
bravery, however, I ſuſpect that they are far
below the whites in perſonal valour. Their
mode of fighting in real war, is a ſyſtem of
ſtratagem, buſh-fighting, and ambuſcade. I
will not, indeed, affirm that ſuch a ſyſtem
alone, though it diſplays no proof of courage,
is abſolutely evidence to the contrary. I believe it is the natural mode of attack and defence, and that the practice of open war,
among civilized nations, is artificial and acquired. It is rather from their abominable and
habitual cruelty to their captives, and, above
all, to women and children, and from the
ſhameful and ſhocking enormities which they
practiſe on the dead bodies of their enemies,
that I infer the deficiency of the Maroons, in
the virtue of true courage. In their treatment of fugitive ſlaves, they manifeſt a
blood-thirſtineſs of diſpoſition, which is
otherwiſe unaccountable ; for, although their
vigilance is ſtimulated by the proſpect of reward,

ward, they can have no poffible motives of revenge or malice towards the unfortunate objects of their purfuit : yet it is notorioufly true, that they wifh for nothing more than a pretence to put the poor wretches to death ; frequently maiming them without provocation ; and, until mile-money was allowed by the legiflature, oftentimes bringing home the head of the fugitive, inftead of the living man; making the plea of refiftance an excufe for their barbarity.

In the year 1760, an occafion occurred of putting the courage, fidelity, and humanity of thefe people to the teft. The Koromantyn flaves, in the parifh of St. Mary, rofe into rebellion, and the Maroons were called upon, according to treaty, to co-operate in their fuppreffion. A party of them accordingly arrived at the fcene of action, the fecond or third day after the rebellion had broken out. The whites had already defeated the infurgents, in a pitched battle, at *Heywood-Hall*, killed eight or nine of their number, and driven the remainder into the woods. The Maroons were ordered to purfue them, and were promifed a certain reward for each

rebel

rebel they might kill or take prifoner. They accordingly pufhed into the woods, and after rambling about for a day or two, returned with a collection of human ears, which they pretended to have cut off from the heads of rebels they had flain in battle, the particulars of which they minutely related. Their report was believed, and they received the money ftipulated to be paid them; yet it was afterwards found that they had not killed a man; that no engagement had taken place, and that the ears which they had produced, had been fevered from the dead bodies which had lain unburied at Heywood-Hall.

Some few days after this, as the Maroons, and a detachment of the 74th regiment, were ftationed at a folitary place, furrounded by deep woods, called Downs's Cove, they were fuddenly attacked in the middle of the night by the rebels. The centinels were fhot, and the huts in which the foldiers were lodged, were fet on fire. The light of the flames, while it expofed the troops, ferved to conceal the rebels, who poured in a fhower of muf-quetry from all quarters, and many of the foldiers were flain. Major Forfyth, who
commanded

commanded the detachment, formed his men into a fquare, and by keeping up a brifk fire from all fides, at length compelled the enemy to retire. During the whole of this affair the Maroons were not to be found, and Forfyth, for fome time, fufpected that they were themfelves the affailants. It was difcovered, however, that immediately on the attack, the whole body of them had thrown themfelves flat on the ground, and continued in that pofition until the rebels retreated, without firing or receiving a fhot.

A party of them, however, had afterwards the merit (a merit of which they loudly boafted) of killing the leader of the rebels. He was a young negro of the Koromantyn nation, named Tackey, and it was faid had been of free condition, and even a chieftain, in Africa. This unfortunate man, having feen moft of his companions flaughtered, was difcovered wandering in the woods without arms or clothing, and was immediatly pur-fued by the Maroons, *in full cry*. The chafe was of no long duration; he was fhot through the head; and it is painful to relate, but un-

queftionably

queftionably true, that his favage purfuers, having decollated the body, in order to preferve the head as the trophy of victory, *roafted and actually devoured the heart and entrails of the wretched victim !* *

The mifconduct of thefe people in this re- bellion, whether proceeding from cowardice or treachery, was, however, overlooked. Li- ving fecluded from the reft of the community, they were fuppofed to have no knowledge of the rules and reftraints to which all other claffes of the inhabitants were fubject; and the vigi- lance of juftice (notwithftanding what has recently happened) feldom purfued them, even for offences of the moft atrocious nature.

In truth, it always feemed to me, that the whites in general entertained an opinion of the

---

* The circumftances that I have related concerning the conduct of the Maroons, in the rebellion of 1760, are partly founded on my own knowledge and perfonal obfer- vation at the time (having been myfelf prefent;) or from the teftimony of eye witneffes, men of character and pro- bity. The fhocking fact laft mentioned was attefted by feveral white people, and was not attempted to be denied or concealed by the Maroons themfelves. They feemed in- deed to make it the fubject of boafting and triumph.

ufefulnefs of the Maroons; which no part of
their conduct, at any one period, confirmed.
—Poffibly their perfonal appearance contri-
buted, in fome degree, to preferve the delufion;
for, favage as they were in manners and difpofition, their mode of living and daily purfuits undoubtedly ftrengthened the frame, and
ferved to exalt them to great bodily perfec-
tion. Such fine perfons are feldom beheld
among any other clafs of African or native
blacks. Their demeanour is lofty, their walk
firm, and their perfons erect. Every motion
difplays a combination of ftrength and agility. The mufcles (neither hidden nor de-
preffed by clothing) are very prominent, and
ftrongly marked. Their fight withal is won-
derfully acute, and their hearing remarkably
quick. Thefe characterifticks, however, are
common, I believe, to all favage nations, in
warm and temperate climates; and, like other
favages, the Maroons have thofe fenfes only
perfect, which are kept in conftant exercife.
Their fmell is obtufe, and their tafte fo de-
depraved, that I have feen them drink new
rum frefh from the ftill, in preference to
wine which I offered them; and I remem-

ber,

ber, at a great feſtival in one of their towns, which I attended, that their higheſt luxury, in point of food, was ſome rotten beef which had been originally ſalted in Ireland, and was probably preſented to them, by ſome perſon who knew their taſte, *becauſe it was putrid*.

Such was the ſituation of the Maroon Negroes of Jamaica, previous to their late revolt; and the picture which I have drawn of their character and manners, was delineated from the life, after long experience and obſervation. Of that revolt I ſhall now proceed to deſcribe the cauſe, progreſs, and termination; and, if I know myſelf, without partiality or prejudice *

* It ſhould not be omitted, that of late years a practice has univerſally prevailed among the Maroons (in imitation of the other free blacks) of attaching themſelves to different families among the Engliſh; and deſiring gentlemen of conſideration to allow the Maroon children to bear their names. Montague James, John Palmer, Tharp, Jarrett, Parkinſon, Shirley, White, and many others, are names adopted in this way; and I think great advantages might be derived from it if properly improved.

SECTION

SECTION III.

In the month of July 1795, two Maroons, from Trelawney-Town, having committed a felony in stealing some pigs, were apprehended, sent to Montego Bay, and there tried for the offence according to law. Having been found guilty by the jury, the magistrates ordered each of them to receive thirty-nine lashes on the bare back. The sentence was executed accordingly. They were whipped in the workhouse, by the black overseer of the workhouse negroes; the person whose office it is to inflict punishment on such occasions. The offenders were then immediately discharged; and they went off, with some of their companions, abusing and insulting every white person whom they met in the road.

On their return to Trelawney-Town, and giving an account of what had passed, the whole body of Maroons immediately assembled; and after violent debates and altercations among themselves, a party of them repaired to Captain Craskell, the superintendant, and ordered him, in the name of the
whole,

whole, to quit the town forthwith, under pain of death. He retired to Vaughan's-field, a plantation in the neighbourhood; and exerted himſelf, by friendly meſſages and otherwiſe, to pacify the Maroons; but without effect. They ſent a *written defiance* to the magiſtrates of Montego Bay, declaring their intention to meet the white people in arms, and threatening to attack the town on the 20th of that month (July). In the mean while an attempt was made on Captain Craſkell's life, and he very narrowly eſcaped.

Alarmed by the receipt of this letter, and the intelligence which was received of the temper and diſpoſition of the Maroons, the magiſtrates applied to General Palmer, requeſting him to call out the militia; which was done; and the General ſent an expreſs to the Earl of Balcarres, in Spaniſh-Town, praying his Lordſhip to ſend down a detachment of the Jamaica dragoons. Eighty men were accordingly ſent, well accoutred and mounted.

The militia aſſembled on the 19th of July, to the number of four hundred; and while

8   they

they were waiting for orders, one of the Maroons, armed with a lance, made his appearance, and informed the commanding officer, that they wished to have a conference in Trelawney-Town, with John Tharp, Esq. (the Custos and Chief Magistrate of Trelawney) Messrs. Stewart and Hodges, the Members in the Assembly, and Jarvis Gallimore, Esq. Colonel of the Militia.

As this message seemed to manifest a disinclination, on the part of the chief body of the Maroons, to proceed to hostilities, the gentlemen above named very readily accepted the invitation, and proceeded to the town the next day (the 20th). They were accompanied by Colonel Thomas Reed, of the St. James's militia, a very distinguished and gallant officer, and a man of the highest honour and character, by other persons of consideration; and also by Major James, whose son had formerly acted as superintendant of the town, who was himself superintendant-general of all the Maroon towns in the island, and was supposed to have more weight and to possess greater influence with the Maroons, than any other man in the country.

The

The Maroons received them under arms.
There appeared about three hundred able
men, all of whom had painted their faces for
battle, and feemed ready for action ; and they
behaved with fo much infolence, that the
gentlemen were at firft exceedingly alarmed
for their own fafety. A conference however
enfued ; in which it was obfervable that the
Maroons complained—not of the injuftice or
feverity of the punifhment which had been
inflicted on two of their companions ; but—of
the difgrace which they infifted the magiftrates of Montego Bay had put on their
whole body, by ordering the punifhment to
be inflicted in the workhoufe by the black
overfeer or driver, and in the prefence of fugitive and felon negroe flaves, many of whom they
had themfelves apprehended *. They concluded by demanding reparation for this indignity ; an addition to the lands they pof-

* It certainly is to be wifhed, that fome little attention had
been paid, by the magiftrates, to the pride or the prejudices of
the Maroons in this refpect. The law however is wholly filent
on this head, and the court had a right to exercife its difcretion.
The punifhment, and the mode of adminiftring it, were ftrictly
legal ; and a white offender in a fimilar cafe would have been
whipped by the fame man.

feffed,

feffed, the difmiffion of Capt. Crafkell, and the appointment of Mr. James, their former fuperintendant.

The gentlemen had certainly no authority to agree to any of thefe requifitions; they promifed however to ftate their grievances to the commander in chief, and to recommend to the legiflature to grant them an addition of land. In the meanwhile, they affured the Maroons they would requeft the Governor to provide otherwife for Capt. Crafkill their fuperintendant, and to re-appoint in his room their favourite Mr. James. With thefe affurances the Maroons feemed pacified, and declared they had nothing further to afk; and the gentlemen, having diftributed a confiderable fum of money amongft them, returned to Montego Bay.

It foon appeared however, that the Maroons, in defiring this conference, were actuated folely by motives of treachery. They were apprized that a fleet of 150 fhips was to fail for Great Britain on the morning of the 26th; and they knew that very few Britifh troops remained in the Ifland, except the 83d regiment, and that this very regiment was, at that juncture,

under

under orders to embark for St. Domingo;
they hoped, therefore, by the fpecious and
delufive appearance of defiring a conference,
to quiet fufpicion, until the July fleet was
failed, and the regulars fairly departed. In
the meanwhile, they pleafed themfelves with
the hope of prevailing on the negroe flaves
throughout the Ifland to join them; and by
rifing in a mafs, to enable them to extermi·
nate the whites at a blow.

The very day the conference was held, they
began tampering with the negroes on the numerous and extenfive plantations in the neighbourhood of Montego Bay*. On fome of thefe
plantations their emiffaries were cordially
received and fecreted: on others, the flaves
themfelves voluntarily apprized their over-
feers, that the Maroons were endeavouring to
feduce them from their allegiance. Information of this nature was tranfmitted from
many refpectable quarters; but moft of the
gentlemen who had vifited the Maroons on
the 20th, were fo confident of their *fidelity*
and *affection*, that the Governor, difbelieving

* Trelawney Town is fituated within 20 miles of the town
and harbour of Montego Bay.

the

the charges againſt them, was prevailed on to let the troops embark as originally intended, and they actually ſailed from Port Royal on the morning of the 29th, under convoy of the Succeſs Frigate.

In the courſe of that, and the two ſucceeding days, however, ſuch intelligence was received at the King's houſe, as left no poſſible room to doubt the treachery of theſe *faithful* and *affectionate* people ; and the Earl of Balcarres, with that promptitude and deciſion which diſtinguiſh his character, determined on a line of conduct adapted to the importance of the occaſion. The courſe from Port Royal to St. Domingo (as the reader is perhaps informed) is altogether againſt the wind, and there is ſometimes a ſtrong lee current; as was fortunately the caſe at this juncture. Theſe were favourable circumſtances, and afforded the Governor room to hope that the tranſports which conveyed the troops might poſſibly be overtaken at ſea, by a faſt ſailing boat, from the eaſt end of the iſland, furniſhed with oars for rowing in the night. His Lordſhip was not miſtaken; the boat which was provided came up with them on the 2d of Auguſt, off the north-eaſt end of Jamaica,

and

and delivered orders to Captain Pigot of the Succefs, forthwith to change his courfe, and proceed with the tranfports down the north fide of the Ifland to Montego Bay. Captain Pigot immediately obeyed ; and by this happy accident the country was faved.

The 83d regiment, confifting of upwards of one thoufand effective men, commanded by Colonel Fitch, landed at Montego Bay on Tuefday the 4th of Auguft. At this moment, although the Militia of this part of the country were under arms, and had been joined by the detachment of light dragoons, the utmoft anxiety was vifible in every countenance. The July fleet was failed; and the certainty that the Maroons had collected great quantities of arms and ammunition, and that they had been tampering with the flaves, and the uncertainty of the fuccefs and extent of their machinations, had caft a gloom on the face of every man ; and while rumours of plots and confpiracies diftracted the minds of the ignorant, many among the moft thoughtful and confiderate, anticipated all the horrors of St. Domingo, and in imagination already beheld their houfes and plantations in flames, and their wives and children bleeding

under

under the fwords of the moft mercilefs of affaffins.

The fudden and unexpected arrival of fo powerful a reinforcement, in the moft critical moment, immediately changed the fcene. But further meafures were adopted. By the advice of a council of' war, compofed chiefly of members of the Affembly, the Governor put the whole Ifland under martial law. A further reinforcement of 130 well mounted dragoons under the command of Colonel Sandford, and a detachment of 100 men of the 62d regiment, were fent down on the 3d : Colonel Walpole, with 150 difmounted dragoons, embarked at the fame time for Black River, to command the forces in St. Elizabeth and Weftmoreland, and on the morning of the 4th, the Governor himfelf left Spanifh Town for Montego Bay ; determined to command on the fcene of action in perfon.

The reader will eafily conceive, that meafures of fuch extent and magnitude were not adopted folely in the belief that the Maroons alone were concerned. It muft be repeated, that the moft certain and abundant proofs had been tranfmitted to the commander in chief,

d of

of their attempts to create a general revolt of the enflaved negroes, and it was impoffible to forefee the refult. The fituation of the flaves, under prevailing circumftances, required the moft ferious attention. With the recent example before their eyes of the dreadful infurrection in St. Domingo, they had been accuftomed, for the preceding feven years, to hear of nothing but Mr. Wilberforce, and his efforts to ferve them in Great Britain. Means of information were not wanting. Inftructors were conftantly found among the black fervants continually returning from England; and I have not the fmalleft doubt that the negroes on every plantation in the Weft Indies, were taught to believe that their mafters were generally confidered in the mother country, as a fet of odious and abominable mifcreants, whom it was laudable to maffacre! The Society in the Old Jewry had made no fcruple to avow this doctrine in its fulleft extent, by caufing pamphlets to be diftributed among fuch of the negroes as could read, and medals among fuch of them as could not, to apprize them of the wretchednefs of their fituation, and to affure them, in language and tokens well fuited to

their

their capacity, *that infurrection was their duty,
and that no cruelties, which they fhould commit in
the exercife of fuch a duty, could be confidered as
criminal* *.

* Having mentioned the name of a very refpectable gentleman (Mr. Wilberforce) I think it my duty to declare, that
I very fincerely acquit *him* of any fuch atrocious wifhes or
intentions as I have imputed to the Society in the Old Jewry.
With regard to this Society, notwithftanding their publick
declaration, that their efforts were meant only to put a period
to the Slave Trade, and by no means to interfere with the
actual condition of the enflaved negroes already in the plantations, I do aver, that they purfued a line of conduct directly and immediately repugnant and contradictory to their
own profeffions. In many of the pamphlets and tracts
which they caufed to be diftributed throughout the Sugar
Colonies, arguments are exprefsly adduced, in language
which cannot be mifunderftood, to urge the negroes to rife
into rebellion, and murder their mafters. In one of thofe
pamphlets, entitled, A Letter to Granville Sharpe, Efq. from
the Rev. Percival Stockdale, the reverend writer, after
pouring forth his earneft prayers for a fpeedy infurrection of
the enflaved negroes throughout the Britifh Weft indies,
exclaims as follows: " Should we not approve their con-
" duct in their violence? Should we not crown it with eu-
" logium, if they exterminate their tyrants with fire and
" fword? *Should they even deliberately inflict the moft ex-*
" *quifite tortures on thofe tyrants, would they not be excufable,*
" &c. &c." This, and much more to the fame purpofe, is
the language of a chriftian divine, addreffed to Granville
Sharp; yet I do not hear that either he, or Mr. Sharp, is in
Bedlam !

d 2   The

The wifdom, decifion, and activity of the Earl of Balcarres, on the prefent occafion, defeated all the projects, and rendered abortive all the hopes of thefe peftilent reformers. The effect of his Lordfhip's conduct thenceforward, on the minds of the enflaved negroes throughout the whole country, was wonderful. Submiffion, tranquillity, and good order prevailed univerfally among them. The circumftance attending the return of the 83d regiment, induced them to believe that Heaven itfelf had declared in favour of the Whites, and that all attempts at refiftance were not only unavailing, but impious.

The Maroons themfelves became divided in their councils. Many of the old and experienced among them, even in Trelawney Town, the head quarters of fedition, recommended peace; and advifed their companions to poftpone their vengeance to a better opportunity; and the whole of the *Acompong* people declared in favour of the Whites. It was determined, however, by a very great majority of the Trelawney Maroons, *to fight the Bucras* (meaning the white people). This was their expreffion. The violent councils of the
younger

younger part of their community prevailed;
moft of whom were inflamed with a degree
of favage fury againft the Whites, which fet at
nought all confiderations of prudence, policy,
and humanity.

The Commander in chief, however, previous
to any hoftile movement, determined to try
once more to effect an accommodation. As it
was evident the Maroons confulted fome perfon who could read and write, his Lordfhip, on
the 8th of Auguft, fent into their town a written meffage or fummons in the following
words:

To the Maroons of Trelawney Town.

" You have entered into a moft unprovoked,
ungrateful, and moft dangerous rebellion.

" You have driven away your fuperintendant, placed over you by the laws of this
country.

" You have treated him, your Commander,
with indignity and contempt. You have en-
deavoured to maffacre him.

" You have put the Magiftrates of the
country, and all the white people, at defiance.

" You

" You have challenged, and offered them battle.

" You have forced the country, which has long cherifhed and foftered you as its children, to confider you as an enemy.

" Martial law has in confequence been proclaimed.

" Every pafs to your town has been occupied and guarded by the militia and regular forces.

" You are furrounded by thoufands.

" Look at Montego Bay, and you will fee the force brought againft you.

" I have iffued a proclamation, offering a reward for your heads ; that terrible edict will not be put in force before Thurfday, the 13th day of Auguft.

" To avert thefe proceedings, I advife and command every Maroon of Trelawney Town, capable of bearing arms, to appear before me at Montego Bay, on Wednefday the 12th day of Auguft inftant, and there fubmit themfelves to his Majefty's mercy.

" On fo doing, you will efcape the effects of the dreadful command, ordered to be put into execution on Thurfday, the 13th Day of Auguft ;

guft; on which day, in failure of your obedience to this fummons, your town fhall be burnt to the ground, and for ever deftroyed.

" And whereas it appears that other negroes, befides the Maroons of Trelawny Town, were there under arms on the day that town was vifited by John Tharp, Efq. and feveral other magiftrates of the parifh of Trelawney, you are ftrictly commanded and enjoined to bring fuch ftranger negroes to Montego Bay, as prifoners, on or before the before mentioned Wednefday, the 12th day of Auguft inftant.

" BALCARRES."

Apprehenfive, however, that this fummons would have but little effect, the Governor at the fame time gave orders that the regulars and militia fhould take poffeffion of all the known paths leading to Trelawney Town from the furrounding parifhes; and the troops arrived at their refpective ftations early on the 9th.

On the morning of the 11th, thirty-eight of the Trelawney Maroons, being chiefly old men, furrendered themfelves to the Governor's mercy, at Vaughan's-field, and frankly

declared,

declared, that, with regard to the reft of the town, they were determined on war. " *The devil*, they faid, *had got into them*," and nothing but fuperiority of force would bring them to reafon.

Two of the thirty-eight were, however, fent back to try, for the laft time, if perfuafion would avail; but they were detained by the reft, who, having fecreted their women and children, *paffed the Rubicon* the enfuing night, by fetting fire themfelves to their town, and commencing hoftilities on the outpofts of the army. The attack fell chiefly on the St. James's company of free people of colour, of whom two were killed and fix wounded: and thus began this unfortunate war.

The Maroons immediately afterwards affembled in a body, near a fmall village which was called their *New* Town, behind which were their provifion grounds.——On the afternoon of the 12th, orders were given to Lieutenant Colonel Sandford to march with a detachment of the 18th and 20th dragoons, and a party of the horfe militia, and take poffeffion of thofe grounds the fame evening; it being the Governor's intention to attack

the

the Maroons at the fame time, in front. Colonel Sandford proceeded accordingly, accompanied by a body of volunteers; but having been
informed that the Maroons had retired to the
ruins of their old town, he was perfuaded, inftead
of waiting at his·poft for further orders from
the Governor, to proceed beyond his limits, and
to pufh after the enemy; a moft unfortunate
and fatal determination, to which this gallant
officer, and many valuable men, fell a facrifice. The retreat of the Maroons from the
New Town, was a feint to draw the whites
into an ambufcade, which unfortunately fucceeded. The road between the new and old
towns was very bad and very narrow; and
the troops had marched about half way, the
regulars in front, the militia in the centre,
and the volunteers in the rear, when a heavy
fire enfued from the bufhes. Colonel Sandford was among the firft that fell, and with
him perifhed Quarter Mafter M'Bride, fix
privates of the 20th, and eight of the 18th
light dragoons. Of the militia, thirteen were
flain outright, and, among the reft, the commanding officer, Colonel Gallimore; eight of
the volunteers alfo were killed, and many of all
defcriptions

defcriptions wounded. The troops, however, pufhed forward, and drove the Maroons from their hiding places, and after a night of unparalleled hardfhip, the furvivors got back to Vaughan's-field in the morning, and brought with them moft of their wounded companions*.

Thus terminated this difaftrous and bloody conflict; in which it was never known with certainty, that a fingle Maroon loft his life. Their triumph therefore was great, and many of the beft informed among the planters, in confequence of it, again anticipated the moft dreadful impending calamities. So general was the alarm, that the Governor thought it neceffary, in a proclamation which he iffued

* Among the officers of the Militia who efcaped on this occafion, was my late excellent and lamented friend *George Goodin Barrett.* He was attended on that day by a favourite Negro Servant; of whom it is related that, during the firft attack, perceiving a Maroon from behind a tree prefent his gun at his beloved mafter, he inftantly rufhed forward to protect him, by interpofing his own perfon; and actually received the fhot in his breaft. I rejoice to add, that the wound was not mortal, and that the poor fellow has been rewarded as he deferved, for fuch an inftance of heroic fidelity as hiftory has feldom recorded. Yet this man was, what is called, *a Slave.*

on the occafion, to make publick the orders he had given to Colonel Sandford and to declare in exprefs terms, that if the detachment under that officer's command had remained at the poft which he was directed to occupy, the Maroons, in all probability, would have been compelled to furrender themfelves prifoners of war. " Soldiers will learn from this fatal leffon (adds his Lordfhip moft truly) the indifpenfible neceffity of ftrictly adhering to orders. An excefs of ardour is often as prejudicial to the accomplifhment of any military enterprize, as cowardice itfelf."—The truth was, that the whole detachment held the enemy in too great contempt. They marched forth in the confidence of certain victory, and never having had any experience of the Maroons mode of fighting difregarded the advice of fome faithful negro attendants, who apprized them of it. Happily the clafs of people on whom the Maroons relied for.fupport remained peaceably difpofed ; nor did an inftance occur to raife a doubt of their continuing to do fo.

By the death of Sandford, the command, in the Governor's abfence, devolved on Colonel Fitch, an officer whofe general deport-

ment

ment and character excited great expectation;
but the Maroons found means to elude his
vigilance. They had now eftablifhed their head
quarters at a place in the interior country,
of moft difficult accefs, called the *Cockpits*;
a fort of valley or dell, furrounded by fteep
precipices and broken rocks, and by mountains
of prodigious height; in the caverns of which
they had fecreted their women and children,
and depofited their ammunition. From this
retreat (almoft inacceffible to any but themfelves) they fent out fmall parties of their
ableft and moft enterprizing young men,
fome of which were employed in prowling
about the country in fearch of provifions, and
others in fetting fire by night to fuch houfes
and plantations as were unprovided with a
fufficient guard. In the beginning of September, they burnt the habitation and fettlement of Mr. George Gordon, called Ken-
mure; and foon afterwards the dwelling
houfe and buildings of a coffee plantation,
called Lapland; the proprietor too fuftained
the ftill greater lofs of thirty valuable negroes,
whom the Maroons compelled to go with
them, loaden with plunder. Another plantation,

tation, called Catadupa, was deftroyed by
them in the fame manner, and ten of the
negroes carried off. About the fame time,
they burnt the property of John Shand, Efq.
a fettlement belonging to Meffrs. Stevens and
Bernard, a plantation called Bandon, a houfe
of a Mr. Lewis, and various others.

At fome of thefe places feveral white people
unfortunately fell into their hands, all of whom
were murdered in cold blood, without any
diftinction of fex, or regard to age. Even
women in childbed, and infants at the breaft,
were alike indifcriminately flaughtered by this
favage enemy ; and the fhrieks of the miferable victims, which were diftinctly heard at the
pofts of the Britifh detachments, frequently
conveyed the firft notice, that the Maroons
were in the neighbourhood.

The fate of Mr. Gowdie, a refpectable and
venerable planter, who lived within a few miles
of Trelawney Town, was remarkable. This
gentleman, having a better opinion of the
Maroons than they deferved, had employed
one of their chief men to act as the overfeer
or fuperintendant of his plantation, whom he
treated with fingular kindnefs, and allowed
him

him the fame wages as would have been paid
to a white perfon in the fame capacity. Although, on the commencement of hoftilities,
this man had joined the infurgents, Mr. Gowdie continued to place a fatal dependance on
his fidelity, and was induced to vifit his own
plantation, as often as his neceffary attendance
on military duty would allow. He had the
moft perfect confidence that his Maroon
overfeer would interfere to protect him from
danger; yet did this barbarous villain come himfelf to the houfe of his benefactor, at the head of
a band of favages, and having coolly informed
Mr. Gowdie, that the Maroons had taken an
oath, after their manner, to murder all the
whites without diftinction, he maffacred both
him and his nephew (the only white perfon
with him) without compunction or remorfe.

But, perhaps, no one circumftance in the
courfe of this moft unfortunate war excited
greater indignation, or awakened more general fympathy, than the death of Colonel Fitch,
who, notwithftanding the recent example of
Colonel Sandford's fate, perifhed nearly in the
fame manner as that unfortunate officer had
done; being like him furprifed by an enemy
in

in ambufh. On the 12th of September, he
went out with a detachment of the 83d regiment, confifting of thirty-two men, to relieve fome diftant out-pofts; at one of which
he left a guard, and proceeded onwards with
the reft of his men; but after getting about
half a mile further, he was attacked by a
volley of mufquetry from the bufhes, and received a wound in the breaft, with which he
dropt. After expreffing a wifh, and receiving
affurances, that he fhould not fall alive into
the hands of the mercilefs favages, he raifed
himfelf up, when another ball took place in
his forehead, which inftantly put an end to
his life. A corporal and three privates of the
83d, and two negro fervants, were alfo killed,
and Captain Leigh and nine of the party
wounded; and if the guard, which had been
left behind, had not pufhed forward to their
affiftance, immediately on hearing the firing,
not one of the whole detachment would have
efcaped with life; two of them actually fell
into the hands of the enemy, and were put
to death with circumftances of outrageous
barbarity, and Captain Leigh afterwards died
of his wounds. The misfortune of this day

was

was aggravated too by a circumftance, which, though fhocking to relate, muft not be omitted, as it ftrongly marks the bafe and ferocious character of the Maroons. When the remains of Colonel Fitch were found, a day or two afterwards, by a party fent to give them the rites of fepulture, it was perceived that the head had been feparated from the body, and was entombed *in the ill-fated officer's own bowels!*

It now became evident, that it would prove a work of greater difficulty, than was imagined, to ftop the depredations which were daily and hourly committed by this horde of favages, and it was allowed that extraordinary meafures were neceffary to counteract their conftant practice of planting ambufhes. Neither the courage nor conduct of the beft difciplined troops in the world could always avail againft men, who, lurking in fecret like the tygers of Africa, (themfelves unfeen) had no object but murder. The legiflative bodies of the ifland were foon to meet, and the hopes of the whole community refted on their councils.

S E C-

SECTION IV.

THE General Affembly was convened the latter end of September, and their firft deliberations were directed to the fub-ject of the Maroon rebellion, with a folicitude equal to its importance. On this occafion it was natural to recur to the experience of former times, and enquire into the meafures that had been fuccefsfully adopted in the long and bloody war, which, previous to the treaty of 1738, had been carried on againft the fame enemy. The expedient which had then been reforted to, of employing dogs to difcover the concealment of the Maroons, and prevent the fatal effects which refulted from their mode of fighting in ambufcade, was recommended as a fit example to be followed in the prefent conjuncture; and it being known that the Spanifh Americans poffeffed a certain fpecies of thofe animals, which it was judged would be proper for fuch a fervice, the Affembly refolved to fend to the ifland of Cuba for one hundred of them, and to engage a fuf-

ficient

ficient number of the Spanish huntsmen, to attend and direct their operations. The employment to which these dogs are generally put by the Spaniards, is the pursuit of wild bullocks, which they slaughter for the hides; and the great use of the dog is to drive the cattle from such heights and recesses in the mountainous parts of the country, as are least accessible to the hunters.

The Assembly were not unapprized that the measure of calling in such auxiliaries, and urging the canine species to the pursuit of human beings, would probably give rise to much observation and animadversion in the mother country. Painful experience on other occasions, had taught them, that their conduct in the present case, would be scrutinized with all the rigid and jealous circumspection, which ignorance and hatred, and envy and malice, and pretended humanity, and fanaticism, could exercise. The horrible enormities of the Spaniards in the conquest of the new world, would be brought again to remembrance. It is mournfully true, that dogs were used by those christian barbarians against peaceful and inoffensive Americans, and the

just

juſt indignation of all mankind has ever ſince
branded, and will continue to brand, the
Spaniſh nation with infamy, for ſuch atroci-
ties. It was foreſeen, and ſtrongly urged as
an argument againſt recurring to the ſame
weapon in the preſent caſe, that the prejudices of party, and the virulent zeal of reſtleſs
and turbulent men, would place the proceedings of the Aſſembly on this occaſion, in a
point of view equally odious with the conduct of Spain on the ſame blood-ſtained thea-
tre, in times paſt. No reaſonable allowance
would be made for the wide difference ex-
iſting between the two caſes. Some gentlemen even thought that the co-operation of
dogs with Britiſh troops, would give not
only a cruel, but alſo a very daſtardly com-
plexion to the proceedings of government.

To theſe, and ſimilar, objections it was an-
ſwered, that the ſafety of the iſland, and the
lives of the inhabitants were not to be ſacrificed
to the apprehenſion of perverſe miſconſtruc-
tion or wilful miſrepreſentation in the mother
country. It was maintained that the grounds of
the meaſure needed only to be fully examined
into, and fairly ſtated, to induce all reaſonable

men

men to admit its propriety and neceffity. To hold it as a principle, that it is an act of cruelty or cowardice in man to employ other animals as inftruments of war, is a pofition contradicted by the practice of all nations.—The Afiaticks have ever ufed elephants in their battles; and if lions and tygers poffeffed the docility of the elephant, no one can doubt that thefe alfo would be made to affift the military operations of man, in thofe regions of which they are inhabitants. Even the ufe of cavalry, as eftablifhed among the moft civilized and polifh-ed nations of Europe, muft be rejected, if this principle be admitted; for wherein, it was afked, does the humanity of that doctrine confift, which allows the employment of troops of horfe in the purfuit of difcomfitted and flying infantry; yet fhrinks at the preventive meafure of fparing the effufion of human blood, by tracing with hounds the haunts of murderers, and roufing from ambufh, favages more ferocious and blood-thirfty than the animals which track them?

The merits of the queftion, it was faid, depended altogether on the origin and caufe of the war; and the objects fought to be obtained by its continuance; and the authority

of

of the firſt writers on publick law, was adduced in ſupport of this conſtruction. " If
the cauſe and end of war (ſays Paley *) be
juſtifiable, all the means that appear necef-
ſary to that end are juſtifiable alſo. This
is the principle which defends thoſe extremi-
ties to which the violence of war uſually pro-
ceeds : for ſince war is a conteſt by force
between parties who acknowledge no common ſuperior, and ſince it includes not in its
idea the ſuppoſition of any convention which
ſhould place limits to the operations of force,
it has naturally no boundary but that in which
force terminates ; the deſtruction of the life
againſt which the force is directed." It was
allowed (with the ſame author) that gratuitous
barbarities borrow no excuſe from the licence
of war, of which kind is every cruelty and
every inſult that ſerves only to exaſperate the
ſufferings, or to incenſe the hatred of an enemy, without weakening his ſtrength, or in
any manner tending to procure his ſubmiſ-
ſion ; ſuch as the ſlaughter of captives, the
ſubjecting them to indignities or torture, the

* Vol. ii. p. 417.

violation

violation of women, and in general the deſtruction or defacing of works that conduce
nothing to annoyance or defence. Theſe enormities are prohibited not only by the practice
of civilized nations, but by the law of nature
itſelf; as having no proper tendency to accele-
rate the termination, or accompliſh the object
of the war; and as containing that which in
peace and war is equally unjuſtifiable, namely,
ultimate and gratuitous miſchief. Now all theſe
very enormities were practiſed, not by the
Whites againſt the Maroons, but by the Maroons themſelves againſt the Whites. Humanity therefore, it was ſaid, was no way
concerned in the ſort of expedient that was
propoſed, or any other, by which ſuch an
enemy could moſt ſpeedily be extirpated.
They were not an unarmed, innocent and de-
fenceleſs race of men, like the ancient Americans; but a banditti of aſſaſſins: and tenderneſs
towards ſuch an enemy, was cruelty to all the
reſt of the community.

Happily, in the interval between the determination of the Aſſembly to procure the Spaniſh dogs, and the actual arrival of thoſe auxiliaries from Cuba, ſuch meaſures were purſued

fued as promifed to render their affiftance altogether unneceffary.—On the death of Colonel Fitch, the chief conduct of the war, in the
abfence of the Governor, was entrufted to
Major General Walpole, an officer whofe
indefatigable zeal and alacrity;—whofe gal-
lantry, circumfpection, and activity, in a very
fhort time gave a new afpect to affairs, and
reduced the enemy to the laft extremity. Although the country to which the Maroons
retired, was perhaps the ftrongeft and moft
impracticable of any on the face of the earth,
it was entirely deftitute of fprings and rivers.
All the water which the rains had left in the
hollows of the rocks was exhaufted, and the
enemy's only refource was in the leaves of the
wild-pine; a wonderful contrivance, by which
Divine Providence has rendered the fterile and
rocky defarts of the forrid zone in fome degree
habitable *; but even this refource was at

e 4 length

---

* The botanical name is *Tillandfia maxima*. It is not,
properly fpeaking, *a tree*; but a plant, which fixes itfelf
and takes root on the body of a tree, commonly in the
fork of the greater branches of the wild cotton tree. By
the conformation of its leaves, it catches and retains water from every fhower. Each leaf refembles a fpout, and

forms

length exhaufted, and the fufferings of the
rebels, for want both of water and food, were
exceffive. By the unremitting diligence and
indefatigable exertions of the troops, all or
moft of the paffes to other parts of the country were effectually occupied; and a perfeverance in the fame fyftem muft, it was thought,
foon force the enemy to an unconditional furrender.

In fpite of all thefe precautions, however,
a rebel Captain of the name of Johnfon, found
means to conduct a fmall detachment of the
Maroons into the parifh of St. Elizabeth, and
to fet fire to many of the plantations in that
fertile diftrict. His firft attempt was againft
the habitation of a Mr. Mᶜ Donald, whofe
neighbour, a Mr. Haldane, together with his
fon, haftened to his affiftance. The elder
Haldane unfortunately fell by a mufket ball,
but the fon fhot the Maroon dead that fired it,
and carried his wounded father in his arms to

forms at its bafe a natural bucket or refervoir, which
contains about a pint of pure water, where it remains
perfectly fecure, both from the wind and the fun; yield-
ing refrefhment to the thirfty traveller in places where
water is not otherwife to be procured.

a place

a place of fafety, where he happily recovered.
—The Maroons were repulfed ; but proceeding to a plantation of Dr. Brooks, they burnt
the buildings to the ground, and killed two
white men who oppofed them. They left
however a white woman and her infant un-
molefted; and as this was the firft inftance
of tendernefs fhewn by the rebels to women
and children, it was imputed rather to the
confcioufnefs of their inability to continue the
war, and the hopes of getting better terms on
a treaty by this act of lenity, than to any change
in their difpofition.

The Earl of Balcarres, as foon as the bufinefs of the Affembly would allow him to be
abfent from the capital, repaired in perfon
to the fcene of action, and it is impoffible to
fpeak of his, and General Walpole's exertions,
in terms of fufficient approbation, or to convey
any juft idea of the fatigues and hardfhips which
the troops underwent, without entering into a
copious detail of the various enterprizes and
fkirmifhes that enfued, and the difficulties they
had to encounter from the nature of the country. The line of operation extended upwards
of twenty miles in length, through tracts and

8   glades

glades of which the military term *defile*, gives
no adequate conception. The caves in which
the Maroons concealed their ammunition and
provisions, and secured their women and children, were inacceffible to the Whites. The
place called the *Cockpits* before mentioned,
could be reached only by a path down a steep
rock 150 feet in almost perpendicular height.
Strange as it may appear, this obstacle was
surmounted by the Maroons without difficulty.
Habituated to employ their naked feet with
singular effect, in climbing up trees and precipices, they had acquired a dexterity in the
practice, which to British troops was altogether astonishing and wholly inimitable. On
the other hand, all the officers and privates,
both of the regulars and militia, from a well-
founded confidence in their chief command-
ers, seem to have felt a noble emulation which
should most distinguish themselves for zeal in
the cause, obedience to orders, and a cheerful
alacrity in pushing forward on every service of
difficulty and danger; sustaiuing without a
murmur many extraordinary hardships; among
which, distress for want of water, and thirst
even to extremity, were none of the least.

It

It was eafily forefeen that a perfeverance in the fame line of conduct, muft ultimately prove fuccefsful; and intimations were at length received, by means of enflaved negroes whom the Maroons had forced into their fervice, and purpofely difmiffed, that they were extremely defirous of an accommodation, on any terms fhort of capital punifhment, or tranfportation from the country. They expreffed a willingnefs, it was faid, to deliver up their arms, and all the fugitive flaves that had joined them, to furrender their lands, and intermix with the general body of free blacks, in fuch parts of the country as the colonial government fhould approve. Although thefe overtures were evidently dictated by deprecation and defpair, it was the opinion of many wife and worthy men among the inhabitants, that they ought to be accepted; and it was faid that General Walpole himfelf concurred in the fame fentiment. It was urged that the war, if continued on the only principle by which it could be maintained, muft be a war of extermination. Some few of the Maroons, however, would probably elude the laft purfuit of vengeance; and thefe would form a central point to which

the

the runaway negroes would refort. Thus hoftilities would be perpetuated for ever; and it
was obferved that a fingle Maroon, in the fea-
fon of crop, with no other weapon than a
firebrand, might deftroy the cane fields of
many opulent parifhes, and confume in a few
hours, property of immenfe value. To thefe
confiderations, was to be added the vaft expence of continuing the war. The country
had already expended £. 500,000, exclufive
of the lofs which was fuftained by individual
proprietors; confequent on the removal from
their plantations of all the white fervants, to
attend military duty. In the meanwhile,
cultivation was fufpended, the courts of law
had long been fhut up; and the ifland at large
feemed more like a garrifon, under the power
of the law-martial, than a country of agricul-
ture and commerce, of civil judicature and
increafing profperity.

On the other hand, it was loudly declared
that a compromife with a lawlefs banditti,
who had flaughtered fo many excellent men,
and had murdered in cold blood even women
in child-bed, and infants at the breaft, was a
fhameful facrifice of the publick honour; a
total

total difregard to the dictates of juftice; an
encouragement to the reft of the Maroons
to commit fimilar outrages, and a dreadful
example to the negroes in fervitude; tending
to imprefs on their minds an idea not of the
lenity of the Whites, but of their inability to
punifh fuch atrocious offenders. It was al-
ledged withal, that the rebel Maroons were
not themfelves ferioufly defirous of fuch an
accommodation. Their only purpofe was to
gain time, and procure an opportunity to get
into better quarters; judging perhaps that
the militia of the country, a large propor-
tion of whom were at the diftance of one
hundred miles from their places of refidence,
would foon be tired of the conteft. Many
facts were indeed related, and fome ftrong circumftances adduced, which gave a colour to
this charge; and proved that the Maroons had
not altogether relinquifhed their hopes of
creating a general revolt among the enflaved
negroes. Such an event however was not
likely to happen, while the country continued
in arms. The difmiffion of the troops, on the
fallacious idea of an accommodation with the
Maroons, would alone, it was faid, realize
the danger.

Fortunately

Fortunately for all parties, this unnatural and d ſtructive revolt, was brought to a happy termination much ſooner than might have been apprehended. On the 14th of December, the commiſſioner who went to the Havannah for aſſiſtance, arrived at Montego Bay with forty *chaſſeurs* or Spaniſh hunters (chiefly people of colour) and about one hundred Spaniſh dogs. Such extraordinary accounts were immediately ſpread of the terrifick appearance, and ſavage nature of theſe animals, as made an impreſſion on the minds of the negroes that was equally ſurprizing and unexpected.

Though theſe dogs are not in general larger than the ſhepherds' dogs in Great Britain, (which in truth they much reſemble) they were repreſented as equal to the maſtiff in bulk, to the bull-dog in courage, to the blood-hound in ſcent, and to the grey-hound in agility. If entire credit had been given to the deſcription that was tranſmitted through the country of this extraordinary animal, it might have been ſuppoſed that the Spaniards had obtained the ancient and genuine breed of *Cerberus* himſelf, the many-headed monſter that guarded the infernal regions.

Whether

Whether thefe reports were propagated through folly or defign, they had certainly a powerful and very falutary effect on the fears of the rebel Maroons, a large party of whom now difplayed ftrong and indubitable evidences of terror, humiliation, and fubmiffion, and renewed their folicitations for peace with great earneftnefs and anxiety. A negociation was at length opened, and a treaty concluded; of which, and the proceedings that followed, until the embarkation of the Maroons for North America, the Minutes of the Affembly fubjoined, furnifh a copious and fatisfactory detail. It is pleafing to add, that not a drop of blood was fhed after the dogs arrived. Here then I clofe this introductory difcourfe. From the account that I have given of the ferocious character, and diffolute manners of the Maroon negroes of Jamaica, the calm and unprejudiced reader will draw the proper conclufion, and perhaps agree with me in thinking, that a wild and lawlefs freedom, fuddenly beftowed on any people on earth, neither contributes to benefit fociety, nor to promote the happinefs of the people themfelves. Many of the features which deform the Maroons, have hitherto

hitherto been fuppofed peculiar to men in a ftate of flavery, which undoubtedly debafes and degrades the human mind, and depreffes its faculties; yet, after the picture that has been exhibited of the extreme of liberty, who will contend that a condition of life, which allows the paffions to rage without controul or reftraint, is a ftate conformable to nature, or conducive to the happinefs of mankind? Men in favage life, or but a little removed from it, can only be made ufeful to fociety, or beneficial to each other, by the ftrong hand of authority. Perfuafion is loft on fuch men, and compulfion, to a certain degree, is humanity and charity.

Of the *policy* of ridding the country of fuch an enemy (admitting the juftice of the war on the part of the Whites) there can be but one opinion. After *fuch* a war, carried on in *fuch* a manner, it is impoffible to believe, that a cordial reconciliation between the white inhabitants and the Maroons could ever have taken place. The latter would probably have continued a fullen fubjugated people, employed only in feducing the enflaved negroes from their fidelity, and ready to revolt themfelves

felves, whenever occafion fhould offer. " No country on earth," fays Rutherford, " would fuffer a body of men to live within its territories, unlefs they would agree to be accountable to its laws, as far as the general fecurity requires." To expect fuch conduct from the Maroons, was to manifeft a total ignorance of their difpofition. Concerning another queftion which was ftarted in Great Britain, when the firft account was received of the difpofal of thefe people, namely, the *legal right* of the colonial government to banifh a fet of mifcreants who had been guilty of felony, murder, and treafon; no doubt, I think, could have been gravely maintained on the fubject; except in times like the prefent, when the bonds of fociety feem every where to be loofened; and when crimes the moft atrocious and abominable (if committed by the lower orders of men againft their fuperiors) meet with apologifts and advocates !

It has been afferted, however, that the Maroons were exprefsly protected againft banifhment, *by treaty*; and the high authority of the gallant officer himfelf, with whom the treaty was concluded, has been appealed to

f   in

in fupport of this affertion. It is indeed be-
coming the humane and generous nature of a
brave man, to fhew mercy to a vanquifhed
enemy; and the gratitude that is juftly due
from the inhabitants of Jamaica to General
Walpole, gives great weight to his opinion.
On a queftion between fuch an authority on
the one hand, and that of the Governor and
Affembly on the other, and under fuch circumftances (independently of the perfonal
refpect and efteem which I bear towards
General Walpole) it would ill become me
to offer any decifion: the Affembly confidered that the General was honourably re-
leafed from his pledge, and that their conduct towards the Maroons was defenfible,
not only on the ground of good policy, but
of ftrict juftice. In fupport of their proceedings, they directed the fubfequent minutes to
be printed in Jamaica, that facts might fpeak
for themfelves; and they are re-publifhed in
Great Britain for the fame purpofe. To the
impartial Publick therefore, they are now re-
fpectfully fubmitted.

POSTSCRIPT,

POSTSCRIPT.

THAT no information on the subject of the Maroons may be withheld from the reader, it is thought necessary to inform him, that soon after the subsequent minutes were printed by order of the Assembly, his Majesty's ship the Dover, with two transports in company, having on board the Trelawney Maroons in number about six hundred) provided with all manner of necessaries, as well for their accommodation at sea, as for the change of climate, sailed from Bluefields in Jamaica, for Halifax in North America, the beginning of last June. They were accompanied by William Dawes Quarrel and Alexander Ouchterlony, Esquires, commissioners appointed by the Assembly, with authority and instructions (subject to his Majesty's approbation and further orders) to purchase lands in Lower Canada, or where else his Majesty should please to appoint; for the future establishment and subsistence of those Maroons, as a free people. The commissioners had orders withal, to provide them the means of a

comfortable

comfortable maintenance, until they were habituated to the country and climate. The Sum of £.25,000 was allowed for thofe purpofes.

The following votes and proceedings of the Affembly, having been omitted in the minutes, are added in this place:

HOUSE OF ASSEMBLY,

Friday, April 22, 1796.

Refolved, *nem. con.* That the Receiver General do remit the fum of feven hundred guineas to the Agent of the ifland, for the purpofe of purchafing a fword, to be prefented to the Right Hon. ALEXANDER Earl of BALCARRES; as a teftimony of the grateful fenfe which the houfe entertain of his diftinguifhed fervices, difplayed both in the field and cabinet; and under whofe aufpices, by the bleffing of Divine Providence, a happy and complete termination has been put to a moft dangerous rebellion of the Trelawney-Town Maroons, whereby the general value of property, as well as fecurity of the ifland, have been highly augmented.

✝

Ordered,

Ordered, That a copy of the above refolution be fent to his honour the Lieutenant-Governor.

Refolved, *nem. con.* That Mr. Speaker be requefted to prefent the thanks of the Houfe to the Hon. Major General WALPOLE, for the fignal fervices performed by him to this ifland, in the late rebellion of the Trelawney-Town Maroons.

Refolved, *nem. con.* That the Receiver General do remit to the agent of this ifland, five hundred guineas, for the purpofe of purchafing a fword, to be prefented to the Hon. Major-General WALPOLE; as a teftimony of the grateful fenfe which the Houfe entertain of his important fervices and diftinguifhed merit, in the fuppreffion of the late rebellion of the Trelawney-Town Maroons.

Refolved, *nem. con.* That Mr. Speaker be requefted to give the thanks of the Houfe to the brave Officers and Privates of the regulars and militia, for their gallant fervices to the ifland, during the late rebellion of the Trelawney-Town Maroons; and that the Commander in Chief, under whofe aufpices they fought, he requefted by Mr. Speaker, to communicate the high

fenfe

fenfe which the Houfe entertain of their diftinguifhed merit.

Thurfday, April 28.

A motion being made, that a Committee be
appointed to enquire and report to the Houfe
the names of fuch perfons as have fallen in
battle during the late rebellion, that a monu-
ment may be erected to perpetuate their me-
mories, and the gratitude of this country for
their eminent fervices;

Ordered, That Mr. Fitch, Mr. Vaughan,
Mr. Mathifon, Mr. Stewart, and Mr. Hodges,
be a Committee for that purpofe.

Saturday, April 30.

The Lieutenant Governor's Anfwer to the
meffage from the Houfe, with the refolution
of the 22d inft.

*Mr. Speaker, and Gentlemen of the Houfe
of Affembly,*

The prefent you have made me, by your
unanimous refolution of the 22d inftant, is ineftimable.

A foldier's honour, with emblem and em-
phafis, is placed in his fword; and I fhall
tranfmit your precious gift to my pofterity, as
an

an everlafting mark of the reverence, the attachment, and the gratitude, I bear to the ifland of Jamaica.

BALCARRES.

The following Addrefs was this day prefented to his Honour the Lieutenant Governor:

WE, his Majefty's dutiful and loyal fubjects, the Affembly of Jamaica, beg leave to offer to your Honour, our moft fincere and cordial congratulations on the happy and complete termination of the rebellion of the Trelawney-Town Maroons.

This great and important event muft be productive of fubftantial benefits and falutary confequences to the country, in every point of view in which it can be contemplated : tranquillity and the enjoyment of our civil rights, are reftored; public credit, fo effential to the fupport of government and to the profperity, if not to the very exiftence of the country, is re-eftablifhed, and our internal fecurity greatly increafed and confirmed.

From all thefe ineftimable advantages, we look forward with confidence to the augmen-

3   tation

tation of the value of property, which is likely
to take place ; and which, in time, we truft,
will compenfate all the loffes and expenditure
of treafure unavoidably incurred in the profecution of the war.

It is with peculiar fatisfaction and gratitude
we acknowledge the lively impreffion made
on us by the energy difplayed by your Lordfhip in difficult operations of war ; which affords the moft convincing proof, that the zeal,
ardour, and activity manifefted in your military
conduct, have only been equalled by the found
policy, and decifive meafures, which marked
the wifdom of your councils.

HIS HONOUR'S ANSWER.

*Mr. Speaker, and Gentlemen of the Houfe of
Affembly,*

Your addrefs excites in my bofom every
fenfation of pleafure, the mind of man is capable of receiving.

The picture you have drawn of the future
profperity of the Ifland, is ftrong and impref-
five.

After

After contemplating the unavoidable calamities of war, a fentiment arifes, grateful and
foothing to a feeling heart—

That, during your conteft with an enemy
the moft ferocious that ever difgraced the an-
nals of hiftory:

That, during your conteft with an army of
favages, who have indifcriminately maffacred
every prifoner whom the fortune of war had
placed in their power—no barbarity, nor a fingle
act of retaliation, has fullied the brightnefs
of your arms.

I pray that the energy, the vigour, and the
humanity, which you have fo honourably difplayed, may defcend to your children; and fecure to them for ever thofe bleffings which you
have hitherto enjoyed, under the mild and
happy government of the illuftrious houfe of
Hanover.

THE

PROCEEDINGS

OF THE

Governor and Affembly of Jamaica,

IN REGARD TO THE

MAROON NEGROES:

PUBLISHED BY ORDER OF THE ASSEMBLY.

L O N D O N:

Re-printed for J. STOCKDALE, Picadilly,
November 1796.

HOUSE OF ASSEMBLY.

MONDAY, *30th November*, 1795.

A PETITION of fundry perfons, known under the denomination of Maroons, was prefented to the houfe, and read, fetting forth,
   " That the petitioners have always been faithful
to their king and country, and obedient to the
laws:
   " That they have never joined in any rebellion
or rebellious confpiracy; on the contrary, they de-
teft and abhor all treafons and treafonable practices:
   " That they are willing and anxious to take the
benefit of the act, and to give up for ever any right
they may have of inheritance to any of the lands
granted to the maroons, wherefoever fituated:
   " That many of the petitioners are totally depen-
dent on the goonefs of the white inhabitants; that
many have children, and have it not in their power
to procure a fettlement;"
And praying for relief.
   Note. The above petition is fubfcribed with the
   following names: *Elizabeth Collins, Francis
   Collins, Margaret Collins, Sally Collins, Joanna
   Graham, Quafheba, Molly, Nancy Grey, Mary
   Simpfon, Elizabeth Palmer, Margaret Reid,
   Amelia Lewis, Peggy Murray, Matthew Tho-
   mas.*

B   THURSDAY,

THURSDAY, *3d December*, 1795.

A meſſage from his honour the lieutenant-governor, by his ſecretary, as follows :

" *Mr. Speaker,*
" I am commanded by his honour the lieutenant-
governor to lay before the houſe a petition preſented
to him from the Trelawny-Town maroons, who ſurrendered to his honour in obedience to his proclamation of the 8th of Auguſt laſt:

' JAMAICA, *ſſ.*
    ' *To the right honourable* ALEXANDER *earl of*
       BALCARRES, *lieutenant-governor and com-*
       mander in chief, &c. &c. &c.
' *The humble petition of the Trelawny-Town maroons,*
    now in the barracks in Kingſton.

   ' *Humbly ſheweth,*
  ' That your petitioners, in purſuance of a proclamation of your lordſhip, of the 8th day of
Auguſt laſt, ſent into the Trelawny maroon town,
ſurrendered themſelves to your lordſhip :
  ' That, by virtue of an act entitled, " An act to
repeal ' An act for the better order and government
of the negoes belonging to the ſeveral negro-
towns ; and for preventing them from purchaſing of
ſlaves ; and for encouraging the ſaid negroes to go
in purſuit of runaway ſlaves ; and for other pur-
poſes therein mentioned ;' and for giving the maroon

roon negroes further protection and security; for altering the mode of trial; and for other purposes," it is enacted, that it shall be lawful for any maroon negro or negroes to appear in person before the justices of their precinct, at the time they shall preside at any of the courts of quarter-sessions, and there and then publicly and solemnly to declare, that he, she, or they, are desirous and willing to give up any right he, she, or they, may have to any part of the lands which have been granted to the maroon negroes, and that he, she, or they, are desirous and willing to reside in any other part of the island, except in any of the maroon towns:

' That your petitioners are desirous to avail themselves of the terms of the said act; but that, in so doing, your petitioners will be without any means of support:

' Your petitioners therefore humbly submit themselves to your lordship's mercy and consideration in the premises;

' And your petitioners shall ever pray, &c.

' *3d November,* 1795.

his
John + James
mark.

his
Joseph + Campbell
mark.

his
Donald + Cooper
mark.

B 2   Cuffie

Cuffie + his mark

James + Ruffea his mark

Herbert + Jarrett his mark

Martin + Sewell his mark

William + Anglin his mark

Witnefs,
ROBERT GIBB.

Samuel + Tharp his mark.

William + Libbart his mark

Daniel + Bernard his mark

John + Euler his mark

John + Witter his mark

Gayton + Quaco his mark

Peter + Gordon his mark

Little

Little + Quaco
his
mark

John + Tharp, *capt.*
his
mark

Robert + Jackfon, *capt.*
his
mark

James + Lawrence, *capt.*
his
mark

Samuel + Shaw, *capt.*
his
mark

James + Williams, *capt.*
his
mark

John + Thomfon, *lieut.*
his
mark

James + Reilly
his
mark

Charles + Bernard, *lieut.*
his
mark

John + Samuel
his
mark

Bob + Downer
his
mark

John Graham

Miles Hall

John Moftyn

B 3

John

[6]

his
John + Sympſon
mark

his
John + Palmer
mark

his
James + Bernard
mark

his
John + Bucknor
mark

' JAMAICA, *ſſ.*

' Robert Gibb, of the pariſh of Kingſton, gentleman, being duly ſworn, maketh oath and ſaith,
that he was preſent and did ſee the above thirty-
three perſons ſet and ſubſcribe their ſeveral marks
or names to the aforegoing petition.

' *Sworn before me, this 5th aay of November,* 1795.
' SIMON TAYLOR.'

her
Sukey + Martin
mark, for ſelf and child, named
William Martin

her
Mary + Sterling
mark

her
Mimba +
mark, and her daughter, Mary
Fiſher

her
Maria +
mark, for ſeif and child, named
Thomas Morris

Patience

[7]

her
Patience +
mark

her
Juba +
mark, for self and her child, named
Quamina
her
Amelia + Palmer
mark
her
Susanna + Palmer
mark, for self and three children, named Eleanor Pal-
mer, Emily Mountague, and
John Pendrill
her
Witness,   Ann + Sewell
JOHN M'CALL.   mark.
her
Lilly + Allen
mark
her
Rosanna + Scarlett
mark, for self and four children,
named John Quick, Eliza-
beth Quick, William Scar-
lett Earle, and John Auglin
Earle.
her
Elizabeth + Borthwick
mark, for self and child, named Mary Sharp
her
Ann + Maclachlan
mark

B 4   James

his ·

James + Allen
mark

her

Sarah + Saunders
mark

her

Elizabeth + Sewell Walcott
*mark, for self and two chil-
dren, named* Ann Weir *and*
William Walcott

her

Betty + Cole
mark

' JAMAICA, *ſſ.*

' John M'Call, of the pariſh of Kingſton, gentleman, being duly ſworn, maketh oath and ſaith,
that he was preſent and did ſee the above ſeveral
perſons ſet and ſubſcribe their ſeveral marks on the
back of the within-written petition.

' *Sworn before me, this 6th day of November,* 1795.

' SIMON TAYLOR.'

WEDNESDAY, 2*d March,* 1796.

A meſſage from his honour the lieutenant-governor, by his ſecretary, as follows:

" *Mr. Speaker,*

" I am commanded by his honour the lieutenant-
governor to lay before the houſe ſundry papers relating to the rebel maroons, from No. 1 to No. 29;
among which papers is contained the correſpon-
dence between his honour and the honourable
major-

major general Walpole, from the period of the truce agreed on by colonel Hull, to that of the furrender of the rebel maroons inclufive, together with the treaty which was made between the honourable major-general Walpole on the one part, and colonel Montague James * on the part of the rebel maroons, and was ratified by his honour on the 28th day of December laft.

" I am alfo commanded by his honour to inform the houfe, *that the rebel maroons* (a very few excepted) *did not comply with the firft and fecond articles of the faid treaty, until the troops were moved in force againft them.*

" I am alfo commanded by his honour the lieutenant-governor to inform the houfe, *that the maroons did not give up the runaways, in conformity to the third article of the treaty.*

" His honour, however, commands me to fignify to the houfe, that he underftands that the furrender of the rebel maroons was received by major-general Walpole, under a promife of fafety of their lives.

" I am alfo commanded by his honour to inform the houfe, that, upon receiving the treaty from major-general Walpole, his honour thought it expedient to convene as many of the members of the council and the affembly, as the circumftances of time and their places of refidence would permit to meet at the king's houfe on the 24th December laft, in order to deliberate upon the terms of the treaty, and to give his honour their opinions

* The oldeft of the maroons, and chief in command.

thereon :

thereon: the paper No. 29, contains the refolution which was paffed at fuch meeting, and which his honour has alfo directed me to lay before the houfe.

No. 1.

Old Maroon Town, December 20, 1795.

' My lord,

' I returned here this evening, and have the fatisfaction to report to your lordfhip the fuccefs of the detachment under colonel Hull. The maroons, by his judicious conduct, were attacked before they difcovered the advanced guard. I need add nothing further to your lordfhip; colonel Hull's report will explain every thing.

' I have the honour to be your lordfhip's moft faithful and obedient fervant, G. Walpole.

' *Earl Balcarres, &c. king's houfe, Spanifh-Town.*

' I muft moft ftrongly recommend to your lordfhip to lay before the affembly the cafe of the family of Cato, a flave of Mr. Vaughan's: He has, during the whole campaign, been a moft faithful guide; it was by his means that we difcovered the retreat of the rebels, and he behaved, by every account, with fingular bravery during the action: He was unfortunately killed by a maroon in an ambufcade, on his way back to bring up the baggage. G. W.'

No. 2.

[*Private.*] *December* 20th, 1795.

' My dear lord,

' Hull has agreed, I underftand, to a fort of truce.

truce. This is the only part which, *entre nous*, I diflike: But, however, for the fake of public faith, I fhall keep it. My intention was to give them terms, but by no means to fufpend hoftilities until they fhould firft lay down their arms. I fhall adhere ftrictly to your lordfhip's inftructions. I underftand that they will furrender on their lives only; wifhing for land to be allotted them to cultivate.

'I have the honour to be your very faithful fervant, G. WALPOLE.

'*Earl Balcarres, &c. Spanifh-Town.*

'*P. S.* I underftand Hull's truce extends only to the poft about here.'

No: 3.

December 22d, 1795.

'MY LORD,

'I have the honour to inclofe to your lordfhip the propofals of the maroons, to which I have acceded.

'The party under Johnftone have been fent to by Montague James, ordering them to come in; but they are not expected before to-morrow, at which time the party here are to come in to build their huts.

'The whole detachment behaved to their credit. I muft not omit to mention to your lordfhip, that to the impreffion made in the action by the undaunted bravery of the 17th dragoons, who were more particularly engaged on the 15th, we owe the fubmiffion of the rebels: The maroons fpeak

of

of them with aftonifhment. Mr. Werge was particularly fignalized with the advanced guard; and
the ferjeant-major of that regiment is ftrongly recommended, for his fpirit and activity, by the
commanding officer Mr. Edwards, who is every
way deferving your lordfhip's good opinion.

'I have the honour to be your lordfhip's moft
faithful fervant,   G. Walpole.

'The propofals of the maroons were as follow:

" 1ft. That they would, on their knees, beg his
majefty's pardon:

" 2d. That they would go to the Old Town,
Montego-Bay, or any other place that might be
pointed out, and would fettle on whatever lands
the governor, council, and affembly might think
proper to allot:

" 3d. That they would give up all runaways.

" I grant the above.

                    " George Walpole, *major-general.*
                                his
            " Montague + James
                                mark.

" Done on Guard-Hill, 21ft December, 1795.
" Ratified at Caftle-Wemyfs, this 28th day of December, 1795.

            " Balcarres, *lieutenant-governor and com-
                mander in chief,*

        " *Witneffes to the within ratification:*

                " G. Walpole, *major-general*
                " Trevor Hull, *colonel*
                " James Galloway, *lieutenant-colonel*
                " Robert Shawe, *lieutenant-colonel*
                                    " Wm.

"Wм. James Stevenson, *lieutenant-colonel*
"James Stewart, *lieutenant-colonel.*"

No. 4.

' *Spanish-Town, December 24th, 1795.*
' *At a meeting of such members of the council and of
the assembly as could attend at the king's house,*
Present,
Earl Balcarres
Hon. Mr. Attorney-General

Hon. Mr. Rodon	Mr. Shirley
Hon. Mr. Speaker	Mr. Redwood
Mr. Taylor	Mr. Fitch
Mr. Vaughan	Mr. Christie
Mr. Cockburn	Mr. Batty
Mr. Cuthbert	Mr. Galbraith.

"It was resolved, That if the Trelawny maroons, according to the third article of their treaty, deliver the runaways that have joined them, and if they, according to the first article of their treaty, lay down their arms, which arms are to be taken away from them, that then, and in such case, general Walpole's secret article ought to be ratified, as far as their not being sent off the island; but that they are to remain in Jamaica, subject to such regulations as the governor, council, and assembly, may think proper to enact in that respect."

No. 5.
Old Maroon Town, December 24th, 1795.
' My dear lord,
' Two maroons (Smith and Dunbar) have come
in

in from Johnſtone's party, to beg the king's
mercy; and the whole are to be in here on Saturday, to conſtruct their huts within our poſts. I
have allotted them a ſpot between Cudjoe-Town
and the Old Town; there they are to remain until
the legiſlature ſhall diſpoſe of them. If I might
give you an opinion, it ſhould be, that they ſhould
be ſettled near Spaniſh-Town, or ſome other of the
large towns in the lowlands: The acceſs to ſpirits
will ſoon decreaſe their numbers, and deſtroy that
hardy conſtitution which is nouriſhed by an healthy
mountainous ſituation.

‘ No doubt, ſome perſons there will be found who
may object to the war being terminated: Let
thoſe finiſh it better, if they can; and, above all,
do not let them talk of the expence of the war, and
yet object to its termination; do not let them
extirpate an enemy at their wine, and then leave
their poſts to keep their holidays. But there is a
better reaſon for finiſhing the war; the impoſſibility
of penetrating the country, if it is at all defended;
or, if you could get through it, of extirpating
wholly the rebels: They will increaſe by runaways;
and, if you deſtroy them to five, thoſe five will be a
rallying point for more runaways to reſort to, and
thus the war be perpetuated for years. Suppoſe
the French were to ſmuggle in a tolerable engineer
to them; could we even remain in poſſeſſion of the
Old Town. There was a runaway of the name of
Bowman, who *alone*, a great ſpace of time, deſtroyed
plantations, and did infinite miſchief. Rely upon
it,

it, my lord, that, after more mifchief and more expence, you muſt make peace in twelve months.
hence : The difficulty will then perhaps be ſtronger,
which I have met with, than it is now ; namely, that
of fear : To expel this from their minds has been
my chief endeavour ; and it was for ſome time before I could bring two or three of them from the
cockpits into the town : If this was to be continued, nothing will wear it off the mind ; and of
crimes, thoſe committed under this impreſſion are
the moſt horrid.

 ‘ In hopes of your lordſhip’s approbation, I
have the honour to be yours moſt faithfully and ſincerely,   G. WALPOLE.’

No. 6.

[*Private.*]   25th *December,* 1795.

 ‘ MY DEAR LORD,

 ‘ I was obliged to accede on my *oath*; I promiſed a ſecret article, that they ſhould not be ſent
off the iſland.

 ‘ Hull wiſhes much to go home with the account ; and he exerted himſelf ſo well on the 15th,
that I ſhould hope you will have the goodneſs to
indulge him.

 ‘ Mr. Werge, your lordſhip has recommended
for a cornetcy, I believe in the 17th; but I muſt
not conceal from you, that to his preſence of mind
much of the peace is owing.

 ‘ Old Montague is, as far as I can gueſs, the
obſtacle to peace, as much as he dares : Some of
                                            the

the maroons were heard to tell him, that they would have peace whether he would or not.

'I am your lordſhip's obedient and faithful ſervant,   G. WALPOLE.

'Hull's diſpatch was miſ-dated the 20th inſtead of the 19th.'

No. 6. [*Copy.*]

'I have received, in Spaniſh-Town, the treaty ſigned by general Walpole and colonel Montague James, and have ratified the ſame: And I do hereby appoint Friday morning, the firſt day of January next, at ten o'clock, for the Trelawny maroons to come in a body to Caſtle-Wemyſs, to perform the treaty.

'Dated at Caſtle-Wemyſs, this 28th day of December, 1795.

        (Signed)   'BALCARRES, *lieutenant-governor.*'

No. 7.

'MY LORD,

'Every thing wears the beſt poſſible appearance: Several of the maroons have been in this day, cleaning out the huts, and more are expected to-morrow. But Palmer, I believe, it will be difficult to get in, even if alive, with the reſt. They ſeem determined to be ſure that no infringement of the treaty will enſue: I read the ratification to three of them, and your lordſhip's letter, aſſuring them, that whatever might be the future diſpoſal of them, that they would be a free people. They were alſo informed of the 500*l.* donation of the aſſembly, to thoſe who had *ſurrendered.*

                                                'I have

I have the honour to be your lordſhip's moſt faithful ſervant, G. WALPOLE.

' *Earl Balcarres, &c. &c. &c. Caſtle Wemyſs,*
' *Five o'clock, 28 December, 1795.*'

No. 8.

' MY DEAR LORD, *December 29, 1795.*

' Some of the maroons are, I learn, bringing in their families ; but there is great reaſon to ſuppoſe that there is a ſchiſm amongſt them : One of them ſent me word, that old Montague is the cauſe ; and I this day hear that poſſibly he may die in the woods.

' I ſhould think that your lordſhip will chooſe, that all thoſe who do come in ſhould be ſent to you on Friday, and that we ſhould attack the remainder. Fowler has begged that he may have a gorget, with ſome inſcription to ſhew that he was the firſt who made peace with the white people. All this will, I think, ſerve your lordſhip : It will clearly prove, that if matters had been held with too tight a rein, none would have come in. At all events, much is gained even by dividing them.

' I have the honour to be your lordſhip's moſt obedient ſervant, G. WALPOLE.'

' *Earl Balcarres, &c. &c. &c. Caſtle-Wemyſs.*'

No. 9.

' MY LORD, *December 30th, 1795.*

" Notwithſtanding the incloſed papers, I believe that many of the maroons are ſincere ; they admit

C themſelves,

themſelves, that " ſome have bad heart." However, Friday will ſhew; and I ſhall move on Saturday againſt them, if they do not come in. Nine
or ten more, in all ſixteen, are here this day, and
have taken their huts.

'I have the honour to be your lordſhip's moſt
faithful and obedient,   G. WALPOLE.
  ' Earl Balcarres, &c. &c. Caſtle-Wemyſs.'

No. 10.

'MY DEAR LORD,   January 1ſt, 1796.
  'I now give the matter up: Only Smith, Dunbar, Williams, and two boys, are here. I ſhall
ſend them to Falmouth to-morrow. I ſuppoſe
that your lordſhip will admit them to the terms of
the treaty upon which they have ſurrendered.

'I fear that our baggage negroes will not be
here in time for me to move after theſe raſcals in
the morning, and that I muſt poſtpone it till Sunday: In this caſe, I ſhall endeavour to ſeduce the
maroons ſtill to keep near us.

'Your lordſhip ſhall hear the reſult as ſoon as
poſſible.

'Should any future parley proceed from them,
I ſhall refer them to your lordſhip.

'I have the honour to be your lordſhip's moſt
obedient,   G. WALPOLE.'

No. 11.
Old Maroon Town, January 4th. 1796.

'MY LORD,
  'I ventured yeſterday to truſt Smith to return
to the cockpits, to bring in his family, which he
did

did in the evening, to the amount of thirteen; three
of them very fine young men; the others compre-
hended his wife and feveral fmall children. He
had (which induced me to truft him) given me a
ftrong proof of his fidelity and gratitude, by a
material piece of information, that one of thofe
who furrendered, in my abfence with your lordfhip,
is a runaway; that this is an experiment on the
part of the other runaways, to try whether they can
pafs for maroons; and by his (Smith's) advice, I
let him return to the cockpits. A large body are
expected in to-day of maroons, and I hope others:
It will take fome days, I fuppofe, to get in the
whole; for they are as miftruftful as poffible, and
each is defirous that the other fhould make the experiment before him. All this will naturally and
conclufively prove to your lordfhip the impropriety
of holding forth more harfh conditions than thofe
now granted: Should there be any perfon fo dull
to common policy and common fenfe, as to think
that another turn of the fcrew would be better, afk
him this queftion: " Is he prepared to fpin out the
conteft till foreign affiftance may arrive?" This
may be followed up by another queftion, " If foreign affiftance arrives, what will be the fituation of
the ifland?"

    ' I am your lordfhip's moft faithful and obedient,
                          ' G. WALPOLE.'

    ' DEAR SIR,
    ' Unlefs a great number of the maroons came in
laft night, or do come in in the courfe of this day,

               I hope

I hope and truft that nothing will prevent the dogs from going out to-morrow.

' I am perfectly with you, that the pin ought not to receive another fcrew; but alfo clear that it ought not to be relaxed.

Should the maroons difencumber themfelves of their women, children, old men, fick and convalefcents, they would acquire a degree of pliability which they have not at prefent, and, by removing from their prefent country into a new one, we fhould be very much cenfured by the ifland for not having made the attack while it was in our power. We cannot ftop the operations of war; I look upon the treaty in the fame point of view with yourfelf; but I fee the danger of not attacking them fo very clear as to induce me to declare, that I cannot take upon myfelf the refponfibility of acceding to a moment's unneceffary delay.

' I remain, my dear fir, yours faithfully,

' BALCARRES.

' *Honorable major-general Walpole,*
    ' *Old Maroon-Town.*

       ' *Caftle-Wemyfs, Jan. 5th, 1796.*'

No. 12.

' MY LORD,   *January 5th,* 1796.

' Nine (additional) maroons, men, women, and children, came in laft night. I have permitted two or three to return this day, to bring in more of their relations: One, however, I fufpect will not come out to us again.

                            ' The

' The Spaniards are, I fear, a little out of temper. If they cannot be kept, it would be better to avail ourselves of the breach of the treaty by the maroons themselves, and to move on; as nothing can be clearer, than that all treaty would foon terminate were they off the island.

' Mr. Stewart will deliver this to your lordship, and can inform you as to every point.

' I am your lordship's moft obedient and faithful fervant,   G. WALPOLE.'

No. 13.
Old Maroon-Town, January 5th.

' MY LORD,

' Old Montague will be with you to-morrow, and, I believe, thofe who are expected to day. Thefe delays are to be fure tirefome to a great degree, but ftill I think that they will be attended with every good confequence.

' I have the honour to be your lordship's moft faithful fervant,

' *Earl Balcarres.*   G. WALPOLE.'

No. 14.
' MY LORD,   *January 5th, 1796.*

' Your lordship's letter dated January the 1ft, 1796, is but now come to hand. Conceiving the purport to be a pofitive order from your lordship to proceed againft the rebels, I fhall lofe no time in doing fo; but you will pleafe to obferve, that the negroes from Trelawny are but now coming

C 3   up

up (Tuefday afternoon) : We cannot, therefore, move before Thurfday at day-break.

' I muft confefs that even from the truce, if the Spaniards can be kept in good humour, very confiderable advantages might accrue ; we are getting an increafe every day, and we have now thirty, a number far beyond what two battles could give us in flain ; and this is owing folely to diftruft : Each is defirous that his neighbour fhould try the white faith firft ; and when one is fatisfied, the way is, that he returns and brings back moft of his family.

' Add to this, the crops are gradually getting in, and we approach to (or rather they approach us) nearer to our reinforcements from England.

' However, on Thurfday I fhall go forward.

' Your lordfhip's moft obedient,

' *Earl Balcarres, &c. &c. &c.*   G. WALPOLE.'

No. 15.

' *December 8th,* 1795.
' MY LORD,   [*A miftake for January 8th.*]

' I have written to colonel Shawe to procure me, if poffible, fome fhoes for the 16th, as they are feveral of them barefooted, and the fupply which I expected are not yet arrived.

' One misfortune will, I fear, occur as to the dogs ; the extreme want of water : There is none, during feven hours march, between the great cockpit and the fpot where colonel Hull engaged the maroons. Smith likewife informs me, that there

there is none beyond the laft-mentioned place, except what may chance to be got from wild pines. If the dogs cannot be got on through want of water, we muft leave them behind; but I fear that it will be impoffible to fupply the poft with provifions, through fuch a length of defile, and fo difficult a path as it muft be, that it takes up feven hours to go only five miles.

'However, we will get at them fome how or other, either with or without dogs; and the beft fhall be done that can by me.

' I am your lordfhip's moft faithful and obedient,

G. WALPOLE.'

' DEAR SIR,

' I was honoured by your two letters of yefterday. Colonel Shawe has collected, I believe, 130 pair of fhoes.

' Surely a very few breakers will ferve to carry water for the dogs: Ten are procured here, and I dare fay fome more may be picked up.

' I fhall return the Smith family to you, in the manner you propofe.

' I fincerely hope and truft that no column fhall proceed againft the enemy without the dogs, until their inefficacy is proved: Such a meafure I know would fet the country in an uproar. My own refponfibility, as well as my opinion and the report I have made to his majefty of the intended operations with the dogs, leaves no other alternative than to give immediate and due energy to the enterprize

C 4   and

and ideas of the country, in fending, at an enor-
mous expence, for thefe dogs. Yours faithfully,

' BALCARRES.

' *Caſtle-Wemys,* 9*th January,* 1796.'

No. 16.

*Extract of a letter from major-general Walpole to Earl
Balcarres, dated January* 11*th,* 1796.

' Samuels, and a brother of Smith's, fet off for
the maroons this morning : I fhall proceed againſt
them, if fome do not arrive by three o'clock to-
morrow.'

No. 17.

O. M. Town, January 12, 1796.

' MY DEAR LORD,

' Two new maroons are arrived, and three that
were in before, and two women. Johnſtone has
fent to me to fay, that he has not been able to prevail on the women, feveral of whom have been
loſt, and only one found fince the late actions. He
defires to know what I have to fay in anfwer to his
meffage : My anfwer is, that I fhall move againſt
him, unlefs twenty men come in to-morrow. I
fhall therefore begin my march at two to-morrow
afternoon, weather permitting, unlefs I hear to the
contrary from your lordfhip. I am, however, apprehenfive that Johnſtone's reply will fcarcely arrive
in time : They beg till four o'clock ; but if I delay till that time, it will be too late for me to move
till next day.

' Your

' Your lordſhip will pleaſe to conſider what I mentioned this morning, excluſive of the poſition ſtated by you; *viz.* Whether we ſhould be the firſt to re commence hoſtilities: Certainly we ſhall not make peace for ſome time to come, after the firſt ſhot is fired.

' I remain your lordſhip's moſt faithfully,
' G. Walpole.

' *Earl Balcarres, &c. &c. &c. Caſtle-Wemyſs.*'

No. 18.

' My lord,   *January* 12*th*, 1796.

' The maroons were ſo terrified laſt night, and begged ſo hard, that I told the man who was to return to Johnſtone, that if they were not able (the twenty men) to reach me by two o'clock, and yet were diſpoſed to keep the agreement, that I would, upon hearing their horn, defer my march for one hour.

' I think that we ſhall not, on account of water, be able to move beyond the great cockpit this night: On farther examination, it will, I fear, not be practicable to carry water enough in breakers for ſo many men and dogs, but we can carry ſome.

' I am, &c. &c. G. Walpole.

' The poſt at Tacky's Bum ought to be immediately re-occupied; if your lordſhip concurs you can iſſue the order.'

No. 19.

'MY LORD, *January* 12*th, half paft two.*

'We had fcarcely moved two hundred yards, when I met a maroon coming from Johnftone, to fay that he would come with his people to-morrow into the cockpit, to make their huts, and begged that I would have provifions for him; and that he would adjuft every point. I have therefore ordered the troops to ftop at the advanced pofts, which is about half a mile on this fide where we meant to halt during the night. If Johnftone will build his huts within our pofts, I fhall permit him to keep his arms till he fees you, then to lay them down. If, on account of the women, he infifts on building them in the cockpit, in that cafe he muft lay down his arms to me.

'In hopes that your lordfhip will not difapprove of my proceedings,

'I have the honour to be your moft obedient and faithful fervant,   G. WALPOLE.'

No. 20.

'DEAR SIR,

'The maroons, with Johnftone at their head, are either ferious, or they are not ferious. If ferious, it can make no difference to them whether they go immediately to Montego-Bay barracks, there to remain until the affembly fhall difpofe of them, or that they are permitted to build their huts in the Old Town, or vicinity : If they are not ferious, we fhall only give them time to get out of our way.

'We

' We are not a match for them in duplicity. We may put our strength in truth and openness.

' I think you may give them an opportunity until two o'clock to-morrow afternoon, to come in, and then to proceed against the remainder. I really am for pushing them hard. We have this day seen the good effects of it.

' Permit me to express the very high sense I have experienced of your punctuality. Although the principle of the order is not discretionary, still I give you free permission to modulate it according to your judgment.

' Yours very sincerely,   BALCARRES.
Castle-Wemyss, Jan. 13th, 1796.'
' _Hon. major-general Walpole._'

No. 21.
Advanced post 17th _lt. dragoons, Jan._ 14th, 1796.
' MY LORD,

' Young Jarrett, and four boys capable of bearing arms, with nineteen women and children, have arrived at the Old Town; but on my arrival here, I found Bonny the maroon dispatched to me by Johnstone yesterday, returned with another message, saying, that he had so many sick people that he could not reach me this day, but would not fail being with me in the morning. This is really so perplexing, that I do not know what to do. Your lordship's directions will reach me time enough, if dispatched immediately, to enable me to proceed part of the way to-night, if your lordship disap-
proves

proves of my waiting till to-morrow; but if, on the other hand, your lordſhip ſhould think it proper for me to wait till the morning, it will certainly be right for me to delay where I am at preſent.

‘ I have the honour to be your lordſhip’s moſt obedient,   G. WALPOLE.’

‘ DEAR SIR,

‘ My orders are,

‘ That young Jarrett, the four boys, Bonny, and the 19 women and children, be immediately ſecured as priſoners:

‘ That you do advance againſt the rebels, at the very earlieſt moment after you receive this order:

‘ That you may take Bonny as a guide, if you chooſe, and take every meaſure to diſcover where the maroons are:

‘ Should the maroons, in a body, offer to ſurrender, you may receive their arms on the ſpot:

‘ Any meſſenger going backwards and forwards is not to delay your operations:

‘ All the maroons now in, to be ſent to Montego-Bay, as ſoon as you can procure a ſufficient eſcort.

‘ I have the honour to remain, with the greateſt eſteem, yours,   BALCARRES.

‘ C. W. January 14th, 1796.

‘ Major-general Walpole.’

No. 22.

Paſt three o’clock, January 14th, 1796.

‘ MY LORD,

‘ Your lordſhip’s orders will be obeyed at dawn, to-morrow.

‘ Your

' Your lordſhip is not, I apprehend, aware that Jarrett ſurrendered under the treaty, two days ſince; and, though charged with a meſſage from me to Johnſtone, ſaid, at the ſame time, that he would return ; and has kept his word.

' Bonny ſurrendered yeſterday, and went backwards and forwards twice this day, bringing in his family: His zeal has, I aſſure you, ſince he has firſt come here, and witneſſed our conduct, been only equalled by his activity as a rebel. I underſtand that he, with Smith, are eſteemed the moſt intelligent among them.

' Old Palmer, Fowler and Taylor, his two ſons, are alſo arrived, all uncommonly fine men ; Briſſett, &c. in all nine men, and about forty women and children ; they ſeem not to care about their arms.

' Fowler, whoſe wife is ſo big with child as not to be able to reach the poſts this day, has entreated me to let him accompany me in the morning, to endeavour to ſave her ; this will not, I fear, be poſſible to do, from the dogs.

' The maroons are where they were exactly : I mean as to reſidence ; for there is this difference, that they are on their road hither.

' I have the honour to be your lordſhip's moſt obedient,   G. WALPOLE.'

' There always will be a difference as to thinking between thoſe on the ſpot and thoſe at a diſtance ; repreſentations never ſtrike the ſame as ocular and even auricular demonſtration : I wiſh

your

your lordſhip was here ; but your orders ſhall be
implicitly obeyed   G. W.'

No. 23.

Old Maroon Town, Jan. 15, 1796.

‘ My lord,

‘ Eleven ſtout able maroons, with five women
and nineteen children, are juſt arrived at this poſt.

‘ I ſend you a penciled note from general Walpole, on his march ; wherein your lordſhip will ſee,
that he has met with, in different parties, between
50 and 60 men, women, and children, and Johnſtone with them ; and that they will be all in ; requeſting your lordſhip's inſtructions further how he
is to proceed.

‘ I have the honour to be, in haſte, reſpectfully,
your obedient ſervant,

‘ G. Browne, *major* 83*d reg.*'

No. 24.

‘ My lord,   *Old Town, Jan.* 15, 1796.

‘ Since my information diſpatched to your lordſhip through major Browne, the maroons have been
coming in till dark. Several are ſtill out ; Smith
would reckon about twenty or thirty ; but I ſhould
think more. The troops ſleep in the woods, between
three and four miles from hence. I ſhall rejoin them,
and move forward, if any procraſtination ſhould enſue in the morning.

‘ The total, ſince the commencement of the preſent treaty, who have ſurrendered, including Montague James, *&c.* ſtand thus ; *viz.*

5   ‘ 91 men,

' 91 men, 111 women, 124 children.

' I have the honour to be your lordſhip's moſt faithful and obędient,   G. WALPOLE.'

No. 25.

' DEAR SIR,

' I give you joy of your ſuccefsful operations.

' I have no orders to give; thoſe which I have already iſſued are exactly conformable to his majeſty's intentions, which have been communicated to me this day by Mr. Dundas and the duke of Portland, per the duke of Cumberland packet. Every perſon that comes in ſhall receive quarter; but you will not relax one moment in uſing every means in your power to cruſh theſe rebels: If mercy can be ſhewn, your own feelings will point the way; but it cannot be extended at the expence of one moment's delay.

' All the maroons who come in are to be diſarmed within your poſts; and they will be conducted to Montego-bay. Jarrett and Bonny, I conceive, have ſurrendered in terms of the treaty.

' I have the honour to be, with much ſincerity, yours,   BALCARRES.

' Caſtle-Wemyſs, Jan. 15th, 1796.
' Hon. major-general Walpole.'

No. 26.

' DEAR SIR,

' I rejoice moſt ſincerely at the very happy proſpect of a ſpeedy termination to the rebellion.

' I hope you have in your poſſeſſion Ruſea, Wallace, and Parkinſon: I ſhould, in that caſe, look to an immediate concluſion of the buſineſs.

' The

' The embers ftill remain; to extinguifh them,
I give you a *carte-blanche.*
' I can affure you, that your conduct will be
highly approved of by his majefty.
' I remain yours faithfully and fincerely,
' *Caftle-Wemyfs, Jan.* 16th, 1796.   BALCARRES.
' *Hon. major-general Walpole.*'.

THURSDAY, 3d *March*, 1796.

Ordered, That the following meffage be fent to
his honour the lieutenant-governor.

" *May it pleafe your honour,*
" We are ordered by the houfe to wait on your
honour, and to requeft you will be pleafed to order
all the maroons who are in cuftody at Montego-Bay,
Falmouth, and St. Ann's, to be fent up to Spanifh-
Town, as foon as poffible, by fuch conveyances,
or under fuch efcorts, as your honour may judge
neceffary for their fecurity, to wait the determination of the legiflature; and that the houfe will make
good the expence attending the fame."
Ordered, That Mr. Murray and Mr. Wedderburn be a committee to wait on his honour with
the above meffage; who returning, reported the
delivery thereof.

WEDNESDAY, 23d *March*, 1796.

A meffage from his honour the lieutenant-governor, by his fecretary, as follows:

M.

" *Mr. Speaker,*

" I am commanded by his honour the lieutenant-governor to lay before the houfe fundry papers relating to the Trelawny-Town maroons.

" Firft parcel, twenty numbers.

" Second ditto, twenty-three numbers.

No. 1.

' Dear sir,

' I have great fatisfaction in announcing to you, that, in confequence of orders which I iffued to major-general Walpole, he moved forward with a ftrong column of regulars, accompanied by the Spaniards and the dogs.

' He had only advanced fome hundred yards, when a maroon delivered a meffage from Johnftone: As he had experienced much trifling evafion, and infincerity, it was judged expedient to move flowly on, merely taking the precaution of keeping the dogs in the rear of the column.

' In confequence of this arrangement of the line of march, which I conceive was both firm and temperate, the maroons, to the number of 260, have furrendered.

' I have in my poffeffion, of Trelawny maroons, upwards of 400 perfons, of whom I count about 130 men. Some of the young maroons are ftill out; but I think we have a near and happy profpect of extinguifhing the embers of this rebellion.

D ' You

[34]

' You will announce this pleafing event as fpeedily as poffible, in the Spanifh-Town papers.
' I have the honour to be, &c. &c. &c.

' BALCARRES, M. C.

' Caftle-Wemyfs, 16th Jan. 1796.

• Major-general Campbell, Spanifh-Town.'

No. 2.

Old Maroon-Town, January 17th, 1796.

' MY DEAR LORD,

' Mr. Mathifon will have informed your lord-fhip of the refult of yefterday. Palmer and Par-kinfon are not yet come in, and there have been fome doubts as to them; but I learn to-day that they will come.

' I hope to difpatch a body of about 200, this day or to-morrow, to Montego-Bay: There does not appear to be the leaft hefitation, either to go down there or to deliver up their arms. John-ftone is more eafily to be brought to a conclufion than any of their chiefs whom I have met with, and he preferves very ftrict difcipline amongft his people.

' I could wifh that your lordfhip would have the goodnefs to allow me to keep fuch a body of them here with me as, from circumftances of the mo-ment, may moft conduce to keep them fatisfied in their minds: There is more in this than moft peo-ple think for; and we are at prefent very great friends. Johnftone has defired that his people may

not

not have rum, and he yesterday punished one man for drunkenness.

‘ I have to thank your lordship for your personal kindness to me, and the approbation that is likely to flow to me from the king. It ever has been my wish to discharge my duty honestly; and although I do not expect that his majesty will ever consider my humble exertions to the disparagement of my seniors, yet I hope that your lordship will not think me unreasonable in requesting, at the termination of this rebellion, your permission to return to Europe, with a view to obtain his majesty’s consent, at a general peace, to a sale of my commission.

‘ I have the honour to be, with every regard and respect, your lordship’s most faithful servant,

‘ *Earl Balcarres, &c. &c.*   G. WALPOLE.’

‘ DEAR SIR,

‘ I am honoured by yours of the 17th instant; and I have not the smallest doubt you will do all you can to realize those advantages we have attained, which are in some degree insecure, until such time as these quicksilver rebels are under lock and key. I merely suggest, that a conversation may arise in the country, that the maroons have not surrendered in terms of the treaty; and as such a rumour may get to the maroons, which would make them uneasy, I wish that their numbers resident with you may be reduced by every means you can devise: Any part of them that you wish to keep in the Old Town will, of courfe, remain, until you fee the propriety of fending them to the coaft.

' I fhall order fome preparations to be made in St. Ann's barracks, for the reception of a party of them.

' At the end of the rebellion, I fhall very eagerly embrace any opportunity of doing what may be pleafing to yourfelf.

'Yours faithfully,　　　BALCARRES.'

' *Caftle-Wemyfs, January 17th,* 1796.'

' Jarrett wifhes much to fee his wife and youngeft child; they may be fent to him: The wives and families of Ricketts, Dunbar, and the others, now at Falmouth, fhould be fent down at the fame time.

' *Hon. major-general Walpole.*'

No. 3.

Old Maroon Town, January 18th, 1796.

' MY LORD,

' I have appointed Mr. Werge to fuperintend the management of the maroons, and Mr. Campbell, of the 13th light dragoons, to act as furgeon's mate to them, till your lordfhip's pleafure fhall be known.

' Major-general Reid has, at my defire, offered to go down to Montego-Bay with thofe who are to depart this day: This will prevent any diffatisfaction on their part, I truft; not that I at prefent fee

the

the flighteft degree of it. Johnftone affures me, that they have perfect confidence as to every thing. He came to me yefterday, to defire leave to fend a party of four maroons to bring in Parkinfon and Palmer, with the remainder; and that, if they failed, he gave up all wifh to protect them, and would leave them to be dealt with as might be thought proper.

'We know perfectly where this party are; fo, my good lord, be not alarmed too much. Smith has offered to go with me, whenever it fhall be neceffary, and treats Palmer and Parkinfon with great contempt. I underftand, from the lift fent to me by major James, that thirty-two are ftill out. This lift fhould, though made at the end of his fuperintendency, appear to be tolerably accurate, as it agrees nearly with Smith's account.

'I muft make another demand for negroes, in cafe of accidents.

'Martial law muft be continued till the legiflature comes to a final decifion as to the fubfifting and fettling thefe people. If my prefent gang of negroes do not run away, as their time is out, I fhall, in cafe the remainder are not in, move on Tuefday after them.

'I am your lordfhip's moft faithful and obedient,   G. WALPOLE.'

' *Earl Balcarres, &c. &c.*'

No. 4.

'DEAR SIR,

'I really think that Smith, and others who you have mentioned, have behaved extremely well.

D 3   ' I think

'I think they may with great propriety be trusted and kept with you, to the extent of any thing within ten; and their families may remain with them.

'But I confefs I fhall enjoy no eafe, until I hear that all the reft are actually at Montego-Bay. I underftand you are getting them away; certainly fome addrefs is neceffary, to execute this effential point without offending them; and I am perfuaded that none of them who have been fent down ought to be permitted to return.

'You have now with you all the negroes that were fent up for the purpofe of re-eftablifhing the poft at Tackey's Bum. I fhould be glad to know as foon as you have fixed the propriety of refuming that poft; and I fhall give the neceffary orders for its being occupied by a detachment from this fide of the country.

'Yours fincerely,

'BALCARRES.'

'Caftle-Wemyfs, 20th January, 1796.

'Honourable major-general Walpole.'

No. 5.

'MY LORD, January 20th, 1796

'Two of the maroons, out of the four fent by Johnftone into the woods, have returned (Sam. James, one of them, having been taken ill), with three men, whom I eafily perceived to be runaways. The other two purfued the track of thofe who are out, and, as the horn was heard this morning, I have ftill hopes they will be brought in.

'Smith

' Smith tells me, that the maroons had, early in the war, a defign to go to a place called Oxford, on Hector's River, about feven miles on this fide of One-Eye, in St. Elizabeth's; but were ftopped by hearing that our troops were there. I hope that Mr. Robertfon deftroyed all the provifions in that neighbourhood; he affured me that he had done fo. I have, however, left Palmer and Parkinfon fhould act upon this plan, ordered the 13th light dragoons to go immediately to Oxford. It muft take up a confiderable time, fhould they do fo, as Smith tells me that it takes a day to go as far as even Vaughansfield from hence; as they are obliged to make three or four trips backwards and forwards for their children; and the wounded are ftill in the woods, who muft alfo be carried.

' Should any of this party come in, I fhall directly fend your lordfhip their names.

' Our negroes are come, fo we can move at any time you wifh for it.

' Any party going hence to Hector's River, muft either go through the pens of Trelawny, or by Accompong-Town.

' I am your lordfhip's moft obedient,
' G. WALPOLE.'

' The two maroons are returned, without finding the others; I fear that they are fcattered about.'

No. 6.
Thurfday, January 21ſt, 1796.
' MY LORD,

' I had the honour of your lordfhip's letter yefterday evening, purporting that an expedition fhould

take

take place, under the command of a fubordinate officer, for particular reafons relative to the field-officers, to take place on Friday next. Having received, through major Browne, your lordfhip's exprefs defire that no expedition fhould take place before Saturday, and that it would be better to continue negociating till that time, I had made the arrangements accordingly; and, if your lordfhip thinks proper, they fhall now continue fo; as I confefs that I fhould not wifh that any thing fhould be attempted of confequence, but under fome of the field-officers; and I have given affurances to the maroons of a little longer indulgence for the coming-in of their families, fome few of whom, from ficknefs, are ftill with the remaining maroons in the woods.

' I fent to major Godley laft night.

' I have the honour to be your lordfhip's moft obedient and faithful,   G. WALPOLE.'

' DEAR SIR,

' I am favoured by yours of this date.

' Saturday, I conceive, will be a very proper day for the expedition, under the command of a field-officer.

' I long to hear of another batch of maroons finding their way to Montego-Bay.

' Yours, &c.   BALCARRES.'

' *Caftle-Wemyfs,* January 21, 1796.'

' *Hon. major-general Walpole.*'

No. 7.

No. 7.

' DEAR GENERAL,

' I muſt uſe one other argument, in addition to thoſe I urged this day, as to the expediency of ſending down the maroons to Montego-Bay; and that is a ſtrong one; namely, That it will be moſt difficult, may ſay impoſſible, for me to meet the legiſlature until this meaſure is effected.

' The ſituation of the maroons muſt be the immediate object of their deliberations, and ſomething muſt be done by the aſſembly as to the diſpoſal of their perſons.

' It will be impracticable for me to inform the aſſembly that theſe people have ſurrendered themſelves, unleſs I can give a much more ſolid proof of it, than the information of their ſkipping about in the Old Town.

' I am therefore extremely anxious that this ſervice may be performed before the return of the dogs.

' Yours ſincerely,

' BALCARRES.'

' Caſtle-Wemyſs. Jan. 22d, 1796.'

' Hon. major-general Walpole.'

No. 8.

Old Maroon Town, Jan. 23d, 1796.

' MY DEAR LORD,

' There could have been no neceſſity for your lordſhip to recur to any argument to enforce your
injunctions;

injunctions; it is my duty to obey them; but certainly I am not fo fortunate as to coincide with
your way of thinking; and my reafon is, that a
very different line of conduct has produced the fuccefs which we have already experienced, and, if
purfued, will probably produce more. The dogs
had certainly nothing to do with it; it was not, I
apprehend, known to the maroons that they were
with us; for the maroons (as I wrote to your
lordfhip I prefumed was the cafe) had moved
the day before we did, and were on their way towards us; we met them early in the morning, about
a mile's march:

‘ I have ordered a lift of forty more maroons to
be made out, to comply with your lordfhip's orders, in the courfe of a day or two: Some few went
voluntarily this morning.

‘ I have the honour to be your lordfhip's moft
faithful fervant,   G. WALPOLE.’

‘ The detachment has marched in fearch of the
rebels.
‘ *Earl Balcarres, &c. &c. &c.*’

‘ DEAR SIR,
‘ I give every refpect to the folidity of your opinion, though it is contrary to my own.
‘ It is impoffible, however, that I can meet the
legiflature, until the perfons of the maroons who
have come in are actually at Montego-Bay.
‘ It is impoffible alfo that I can carry into effect
thofe commands which have been given to me by
his

his majefty, and which are rather of a fecret nature.

' When I enforce the meafure of fending thefe maroons to Montego-Bay, I furely take off from you all refponfibility refpecting the bad effects of our taking fuch a ftep, for which I am alone anfwerable.

' 1 therefore moft earneftly and moft pointedly requeft, that all the maroons may be fent to Montego-Bay, previous to the return of the dogs, excepting only a few, which you may keep, as being ufeful to you, as defcribed in my letter to you of the 20th inftant.

' I remain yours very fincerely, BALCARRES.'
' Caftle-Wemyfs, Jan. 23d, 1796.
' Hon. major-general Walpole.'

No. 9.
Old Maroon Town, Jan. 23d, 1796.

' My LORD,

' Another batch of maroons have juft fet off for Montego Bay; among them, twenty men. I reckon feventy men there before ; which, together with a few that went one day at their own defire, makes from ninety to one hundred men, capable of bearing arms Samuels, with fome women belonging to thofe at the Point, and a brother or two of Dunbar's, will go down to-morrow.

' I have the honour to be your lordfhip's moft faithfully,   G. WALPOLE.'

' With

' With the affiftance of Smith, I begin to guefs at the fpot where the body now out are; but we muft take a little time to confider; I do not like to be beaten.

' Your lordfhip will excufe my requefting of you to permit the inclofed to be fent to Kingfton with your difpatch.'

No. 10.

Old Maroon Town, January 24th, 1796.

' MY LORD,

' Thirty men, twenty-one women, and fixteen children, fet off this morning for Montego-Bay. I intend to fend fome more on the day after to-morrow. There was no fort of difficulty in managing the bufinefs.

' Having given them an affurance, that, whenever they were marched to any place, that I would permit them to carry their arms in their hands, it was intimated to them again this morning; fome wifhed to do fo, others were wholly indifferent; however, Johnftone the maroon fettled the matter, by telling them that they had made peace, and therefore had no occafion for them : The arms were confequently left behind, without the leaft trouble to me, or any wifh expreffed on my part about the matter.

' I have the honour to be your lordfhip's moft faithful and obedient,

G. WALPOLE.'

' Your lordfhip muft be fo good as not to reftrict me to a day, as it is not always that I have a
proper

proper perfon to go along with the maroons off
duty.

' I left colonel Skinner yefterday, about four
miles from hence. I fhould not have returned,
but from your lordfhip's letters. I do not expect
the return of the detachment till to-morrow, at the
earlieft.'

No. 11.

' My lord,   24th January, 1796.
' There are two women of Accompong-Town
here; one of them married into this town; the
other, I fancy, was on a vifit here when the town
was burnt : They are very defirous of going to
Accompong; they tell me, that when on their
way from hence, in Auguft laft, they were brought
back againft their own confent.

' Your lordfhip will be fo good as to inftruct
me upon this.

' I have the honour to be your lordfhip's moft
obedient,   G. Walpole.'

No. 12.

' My lord,   January 26th, 1796.
' Smith the maroon thinks he can find thofe
who are ftill out, and he propofes either to go with
me or without me, taking eight maroons. He is
pofitive that they will rifque no engagement, and
relies chiefly on perfuading them to come in.
This will benefit us either way; as, if we find where
they are, and the perfuafion fails, we can then purfue.

' I requeft

' I requeſt your lordſhip's orders, and have the honour to be your very obedient and faithful ſervant,   G. WALPOLE.'

' *Earl Balcarres, &c. &c. &c:*'

' DEAR SIR,

' I had the pleaſure of your two letters laſt evening.

' We have already ſecured advantages beyond either my own expectations, or any formed by the country. I have already realized every thing pointed out to me, in my inſtructions from his majeſty. To allow eight maroons to go into the woods, to endeavour to perſuade people to come in, who you yourſelf could not prevail upon, would be in contradiction to the ſpirit of my orders.

' I am much afraid that you have not been able to carry into execution my orders, of ſending down the maroons to Montego-Bay. The delay is of the higheſt inconvenience, as it is impoſſible that I can proceed in writing my diſpatches to government, until that duty is executed ; nor can the packet be permitted to ſail until I am enabled to make my report to the king.

' The opinions of his majeſty's confidential ſervants are fixed and determined on the principles of carrying on this war. I feel and I know that I am acting with them, in the orders I have given on the ſubject of ſending the maroons to Montego-Bay. Nothing can be left, under theſe circumces, to your diſcretion. My orders therefore are,

' That

' That the maroons be fent down immediately to Montego-Bay, and to be delivered over to major-general Palmer, or the officer commanding at that poft. If you wifh to keep a few men with you, agreeable to my letters of the 20th and 23d, you may; but even that goes much againft my inclination.

' The two women who fay they belong to Accompong, I think you had beft fend down to Montego-Bay, unlefs you have made them fome promife, in confequence of receiving my letter of yefterday concerning them.

' I think that the maroons fhould be fent down when the dogs are out, not when the dogs are in.

' My wifh therefore is, that one half of the dogs fhould be fent on the road towards Mocho, on Friday morning, and the other half on the road towards Tackey's, on the fame morning. They ought to march by moon-light.

' Soon after day-break, in the fame morning, I wifh that fuch of the maroons as have not been forwarded to Montego-Bay, be fent off; they may halt that evening (Friday) at John's Hall; and I have given orders to colonel James to fend a party of the St. James's militia to receive them at John's Hall on Friday.

' I am, &c. &c.

BALCARRES.'

' *January* 27*th*, 1796.'

' *Honourable major-general Walpole.*'

No. 13.

No. 13.

' My lord,

' Colonel Skinner returned this day, after a moſt toilſome march, in which he went far beyond the ground on which the action of the 13th of December was fought. It does not appear, that the rebels had been any where lately in the vicinity of the route which he purſued.

' I have the honour to be your lordſhip's moſt faithful ſervant,   G. Walpole.'

' *Old Maroon Town, January* 26th, 1796.

' Colonel Skinner ſpeaks highly of the activity and utility of the Spaniards and their dogs.'

No. 14.

Old Maroon Town, January 27th, 1796.

' My lord,

' l have this moment the honour of your lordſhip's letters No. 1 and 2. The orders contained .in thoſe letters I ſhall proceed to put into execution, as directed therein; but I will not anſwer to your lordſhip that the Spaniards will conſent to divide the dogs, or themſelves ; and my reaſon for thinking thus is, I made the requeſt once, and they refuſed it: But I ſhall aſk again; at all events, there may be a feint made towards Mocho.

' I am concerned that I did not receive the alterations of your lordſhip's ſentiments reſpecting the women of Accompong-Town ſooner, as I have permitted them to depart about fours ago.

' About

' About twenty (I have not the lift by me, major Brent having gone with the party of maroons to Montego-Bay this morning) of the maroons are now here ; they confift chiefly of Smith's and Johnftone's families ; and I did fuppofe that it had been left to my difcretion to have retained that number, for political reafons, arifing, to my knowledge, from local circumftances ; but they can be fent down on Friday, if your lordfhip fhould not alter your opinion. I am not clear at this inftant how our effective force ftands, and whether it will enable me to detach towards Mocho, and, at the fame time, leave me fufficient for an efcort to the maroons.

' I fay, effective force ; as thofe which returned yefterday had undergone more fatigue, and had traverfed more ground, than will eafily be credited. Your lordfhip would, I apprehend, wifh, that if any point fhould be given up, it is the march in the direction of Mocho: But I truft that I fhall be able to execute both.

' I fhall inform your lordfhip to-morrow morning, if I cannot.

' I have the honour to be your lordfhip's moft faithfully,   G. WALPOLE.

' A fmoke was feen this day at a great diftance, in the direction of Mouth-River, whereabouts it joins Hector's River, on a hill on this fide, fuppofed to be fourteen miles off.   I believe, from the manner of it, that it was a deception or a fignal, as it was evidently meant to be as confpicuous as poffible.

E   ' When

' When I mentioned, in a former part of my letter, about the number of maroons here, I spoke only of the men.

I thank your lordship for leaving nothing to my discretion ; discretionary orders are too apt to be civil, and consequently not very precise. Your lordship will have the goodness to say whether any, and how many, maroons may be left here. I fear that your lordship did not entirely read my letter, as to any party of them going out.

' I have the honour to be, &c.

'G. WALPOLE.

' I have to thank your lordship for my rank in the West-Indies, as it appears in the Gazette.'

' DEAR SIR,

' I have ordered a detachment of militia, consisting of sixty men, under the command of lieutenant-colonel Shawe, to be at the Old Maroon Town to-morrow night.

' This column is intended to accompany that part of the dogs which goes to Tacky's ; and as lieutenant-colonel Shawe has a thorough knowledge of that district of country, he will explore the part of of it that lies between Tacky's and Green-Vale, following nearly lieutenant-colonel Stevenson's last track.

' He will be out three days, and the dogs will return the fourth day.

' As to the part of the dogs that go on Friday morning towards Mocho, you may either make
that

that an effective movement, provided you can properly support it, or make it merely a feint, to enable you to get away the maroons in the manner I have mentioned, which is my principal object.

' I am, &c. &c.   BALCARRES.'

' *Honourable major-general Walpole.*'

No. 15.

' MY LORD,   *Jan.* 28*th*, 1796.

' I shall move the post on at Coldspring to-morrow towards Mocho, by way of feint, it would be a very great distance from hence, nine miles at least, and then eight more to the spot where the rebels used to frequent. But your lordship may, I think, rest assured, that none of them are on that side : They may perhaps go that way on excursions to burn the canes, but not by intent to reside there. Even Johnstone's party did not like the ground, thinking it not sufficiently rocky and difficult for their purposes.

' Smith was desirous that his brothers should go down to the Point, to see his father, and that the two former should remain there for a few days, in the room of his father and the other brother who is there. Whether your lordship will consent to this sort of thing I cannot say, or whether, if not, you have any objection to their going down and returning.

' I have the honour to be your lordship's most faithful,   G. WALPOLE.'

' *Earl Balcarres,* &c. &c. &c.

E 2   ' DEAR

[52]

'DEAR SIR,

'I have received your letter of this date.

'I really should think that the request of Smith is attended with every danger; and the refusal of it is also disagreeable.

'If it was not for a respect and delicacy I have for your opinion, I should at once say, Make a clean sweep, and send them all down.

'Yours, &c.   BALCARRES.'
'Dromilly, January 28th, 1796.
'Honourable major-general Walpole.'

No. 16.

'MY LORD,   January 28th, 1796.

'The Spaniards are desirous to be permitted to go out alone some time or other; and they mean to remain in the woods until they have finished the business.

'I understand from Johnstone, that there are several runaways in the woods between Mocho and St. Elizabeth's, but not any maroons.

'I have the honour to be your lordship's most faithful servant,   G. WALPOLE.'

'Johnstone and Smith have again assured me, that if I will go with them, or Skinner, they think that every man now out may be brought in: They will go with soldiers, but not dogs.

'No smoke observable on the hill near Mouth River this day.

'Earl Balcarres, &c. &c.'

DEAR

‘ DEAR SIR,

‘ My fentiments are long ago made up upon this bufinefs: Smith's application to day, and their propofal fince to go out without the dogs, all convince me that we have not a moment to lofe.

‘ The beft and moft agreeable news that could poffibly reach me to-morrow forenoon, would be to hear that all the maroons were fecured, and marched off to Montego Bay ; and, in my letters home, I have abfolutely reported that we had fecured them ; of courfe, I muft be on thorns until that moment arrives.

‘ Yours fincerely,   BALCARRES.’

‘ Dromilly, Thurfday, 28th January, 1796.

‘ Hon. major-general Walpole.’

No. 17.

Old Maroon Town, January 29th, 1796.

‘ MY LORD,

‘ In obedience to your lordfhip's orders, received this morning, I have fent the maroons down to Montego Bay.

‘ I cannot but lament that the opportunity (as far as I am capable of judging) of bringing in thofe at prefent out, fhould be thus loft. Pofitive I am, that, had your lordfhip had the fame opportunity of judging on the fpot that I have, you would have been of the fame opinion, and the war probably terminated.

E 3

‘ From

' From the information which I received from Smith, there seems to be but little chance of any but a maroon difcovering a maroon, whenever thefe people are where they can remain quiet for any time. Dogs cannot fcent, but on a recent ftep; and I fear that the maroons are now fo deep in the woods, that no expedition can be fupported againft them, without rifquing a failure of food and water for thofe animals; with a great probability, even if it could be fuftained, of never finding the enemy. Had we accompanied Smith, we fhould, if they had not been induced to furrender, at all events have difcovered where they were, and then could have purfued them. The die is caft, and it is now too late, unlefs they difcover themfelves; for I am told that the Spaniards fay, that they could live in thefe woods for ever, that they never faw fuch woods for fuftenance any where.

' Your lordfhip will be fo good as to let me have your orders; but I could wifh that nothing fhould be left to my difcretion.

' I have the honour to be your lordfhip's moft faithful and obedient,   G. Walpole.

' A fick woman or two, and two children, have been left behind of the maroons at this place.

' I propofe to go to Montego Bay to-morrow, to infpect their fituation.

' I fear that the party will not get beyond John's Hall this night, owing to the number of women and children.

' *Earl Balcarres*, &c. &c, &c.'

No.

No. 18.

Old Maroon Town, January 31*ft*, 1796.

'My lord,

' Yefterday I went down to Montego Bay, for the purpofe, as I had the honour to inform your lordfhip, of infpecting the fituation of the maroons there.

' The barracks are, from the numbers, very much crowded; and I fhould be apprehenfive that fome diforders may break out among the people there. To obviate this, I fhould fubmit to your lordfhip, whether it may not be proper to fit up with boards the underneath part of the barrack, which has hitherto ferved as a ftable.

' Should your lordfhip approve of this, you can iffue an order to the commiffioners for the purpofe.

' I have the honour to be your lordfhip's moft faithful and obedient, G. Walpole.'

No. 19.

Old Maroon Town, January 31*ft*, 1796.

' My lord,

' On the embarkation of the 13th, 21ft, and 49th, I found our ftrength here not fufficient to allow us to fend any of the regular troops from hence down to Montego Bay; and as at that time there was every appearance of a termination of hoftilities, I ordered the detachment of the 83d regiment, then at Great River and its neighbourhood, down to the former place; but as that fide of the country may

E 4 be

be confiderably expofed thereby at the prefent moment, I fhould fubmit to your lordfhip whether or
not it might be proper to order back the 83d to
their original pofition, and direct colonel James to
call in about feventy of the militia to the Bay, to
guard the maroons.

'It will be neceffary to have a poft at Mocho,
about half way between Coldfpring and Catadupa;
the diftance being about nine miles from the firft
to the latter place.

'We muft, I fear, call for a confiderable number
of pioneers; I fhould think about one thoufand, or
twelve hundred; in order to get with all poffible
difpatch through the remainder of the work.

'I much fear that the 13th and 14th will not be
a very active reinforcement for the firft three weeks
after they land, from their having been fo many
months on board the tranfports: I fhould recommend to your lordfhip their being brought up into
the country, in a very few days after their being
landed.

'I have the honour to be your lordfhip's moft
faithful and obedient,   G. WALPOLE.'

'DEAR SIR,
'I am rejoiced to find that all the maroons are
now fecured; but I am forry that your judgment
has differed with mine on the propriety of that meafure.

'Your requifition of twelve hundred negroes, I
am afraid, will ftartle the country, who believe, and
4   I think

I think with reafon, that their efforts to crufh this
rebellion have nearly fucceeded, and that they may
look with fome reafonable hope of their being fuf-
fered to go on with their crop, in a degree of tranquillity and repofe.

'Baggage negroes will be required, as ufual, to
attend any columns which you may fend out; but
if the 1,000 or 1,200 pioneers are wanted for the
purpofe of making roads and communications, I
am of opinion that fuch a meafure fhould be done
by an act of the legiflature, and not without it. I
cannot, however, judge of it, as you have not mentioned the fpecific, or even the general, purpofe for
which they are wanted.

'With refpect to the active operations of the
war, our opinions have gone hand in hand; but
although we cannot be too watchful to fmother the
embers of rebellion, ftill I think you give much
more confideration to the prefent ftate of the war,
than either I do or the country does.

'My general notion of it is, that, the inftant the
reinforcement arrives, the militia may go home; if
a further reinforcement is neceffary, I think it
fhould be dogs:

'That the duty of the regulars will be to guard
the maroon prifoners at the pofts of Montego Bay,
Falmouth, and St. Ann's which laft place fome of
the prifoners fhould be fent to from Montego Bay:

'That the troops fhould be fo pofted as to be
able to furnifh a column to move to any point
where the rebels may appear, in a very fhort fpace
of

of time: Three pofts are very evident, as being
confonant with this idea; namely, Mocho, Dromilly, Old Town, and Vaughansfield. I fhould
have liked a divifion of the dogs to have been at
each of thefe places; but, at all events, Dromilly
ought to be a poft for one divifion of them.

'My fituation in this country, and the neceffity
I am under to attend perfonally when there is a
meeting of the legiflature, muft confine me much
to the fixing of general principles, which are founded both upon my inftructions, public and private,
from the king and his confidential fervants, but alfo
regulated by what relates to the civil government
of the ifland. I know how pleafant it is to an officer to act under direct orders; the next pleafant
circumftance is, to have the greateft latitude given,
confiftent with the abfolute duty of the commander
in chief or governor. But your requeft to have
nothing left to your difcretion, is totally incompa-
tible with the very high fituation in which you are
placed: I muft leave much to your difcretion, as
having the chief command in my abfence; and the
great opinion I have had of the proper exercife of
that difcretion, affuredly will juftify the favourable
report I have made to his majefty of your fervices
in this war.

'I beg you will fend me a return of the number
of arms that were brought in and furrendered by the
maroons; fixteen of which were brought down to
Caftle Wemyfs, by the men that were forwarded to
Falmouth.

'I have

'I have the honour to be, dear fir, yours fincerely,   BALCARRES.'
            'Dromilly, 1ſt February 1796.
'Hon. major-general Walpole.'

No. 20.

Old Maroon Town, 31ſt January, 1796.
'MY LORD,

'As near as I can recollect, the number of arms
delivered in here and at Caſtle-Wemyſs are 95;
of this about 29 are at Montego-Bay. The firſt
party which were ſent having their arms by per-
miſſion from me, they were again delivered up
there, in charge of the 83d regiment. I permitted
one of theſe arms, which had been the property of
a gentleman, to be delivered to a friend of his.

'I called for the negroes chiefly for the purpoſe
of making roads, and eſtabliſhing poſts in advance:
Among theſe, Pond River, the laſt ſtand of the
maroons, it was my deſign to take poſt at, on account of the water; and thence the road might be
continued to Hector's River. This would in a
great meaſure reach the pariſh of Trelawny, and
cut off the acceſs to that plentiful ſupply of ſprings
between the interior parts of the cockpits, and the
proviſion-grounds of that pariſh, as well as open
the communication, down the banks of the above-
mentioned river, with St. Elizabeth.

'As to my opinion, it is of mighty little conſe-
quence, eſpecially when the matter which was the
                                            cauſe

caufe of it may be poffibly paft: But I did, I confefs, think that, by Smith's affiftance, we fhould
have traced the maroons; and had we failed in
bringing them in, we fhould at all events have
known their haunts, and might have purfued them.
What gave rife to the fuggeftion of Smith was this;
the finding a ftick at Pond River, with a white
ftreamer faftened to it. This was one of their fig-
nals; and Smith turning to me, in the prefence of
colonel Skinner, faid, "Sir, we can bring them
out as eafy as to kifs your hand." Your lordfhip
will recollect, that this party of eight maroons was
to have been attended by a party of the king's
troops.

‘ I am extremely obliged to your lordfhip for
your favourable mention of my fervices: I have
but one motive; that of doing what I ought to do.

‘ I muft repeat, that if your lordfhip had had
the different communications, and conferences on
the fpot, that you would then have been more of
my opinion.

‘ I fhall fend your lordfhip an exact lift of the
maroon arms foon; you will inform me if you are
in hafte about it, as I muft go or fend to Montego
Bay.

‘ I have the honour to be your lordfhip's moft
faithful and obedient,

G. WALPOLE.’

‘ *Earl Balcarres, &c. &c. &c.*’

No. 1.

No. 1.

Old Maroon Town, February 1st, 1796.

' MY LORD,

' I have the honour to enclofe to your lordfhip two letters which I received laft night. The maroons, I am pretty certain, went to Oliphant's by the road, and not through the cockpits.

' I have the honour to be your lordfhip's very faithful and obedient fervant,

'G. WALPOLE.

' The 13th dragoons, thirty in number, have been at One Eye during the laft week paft.'

' SIR, *One Eye, January 29th 1796.*

' I am favoured with your orders of the 26th inftant, and am much flattered by the confidence you have repofed in me. I have communicated the fame to major Shawe, commanding the Vere detachment at Hector's River; and have from him received affurances of his cordially co-operating with your orders, and in every meafure will, I am affured, ufe every exertion to crufh our favage foe. I am at the fame time under much concern to reprefent the fituation of the troops at Hector's River and its vicinity: That, for want of neceffary fupplies, the dragoons at One Eye cannot be advanced into the woods; that the fupplies for the Vere detachment at Hector's River are very precarious, they being often in want of bread-kind, and other neceffaries of life; that this want of fupply is owing to a fupinenefs in fome of the commiffioners,

under

under a perfuafion that no maroons will ever make that way. Major Shawe and myfelf waited on colo-lonel Peart, who promifed to exert himfelf to pro-cure and forward provifions, &c. but I fear it will be fome time before we can march, having neither pioneers or baggage negroes for the 13th dragoons. The place alluded to in your letter, as the intended retreat of the maroons, is called Oliphant's, for-merly the property of David lord Oliphant; and fo far from the Trelawny maroons being under any difficulty in finding their way to it through the cockpits, that fourteen or fifteen of them were en-tertained by Mr. Mure's gardener at that place, a few weeks previous to the breaking out of this re-bellion. However, that place is in the poffeffion of the Vere troops on Hector's River banks. If I had been furnifhed with the neceffary fupplies and baggage negroes, I intended to have fcoured the woods acrofs the country, by way of Mouth River, home to the Trelawny fettlements.

' The Vere detachment have been immured in the woods ever fince the 20th November 1795. This they have all along fubmitted to without a murmur; the fervice has to them been peculiarly fevere, owing to the remote fituation from their homes, which prevented them drawing fupplies from their friends. However, they have no wifh but for the public good, and wait with anxiety the moment to call them to action. Neverthelefs, it would be an act of charity to relieve them, or change their poft.

' I remain

' I remain, with the greateſt reſpect, ſir, your moſt obedient and very. humble ſervant,

' *Hon. major-general Walpole,* FRAS. ROBERTSON.'

' *Old Maroon Town.*'

' SIR,

' I received your favour, and ſhall certainly be- nefit all I can from Mr. Robinſon's information, and will co-operate with much pleaſure in any thing that may be deemed neceſſary for the good of the ſervice we are engaged in. From every inform- ation I have had from colonel Batty and general Campbell, I have been always led to believe the ma- roons were likely to be drove in here; and colonel Batty, in a former letter, adviſed me to ſolicit colo- nel Peart to ſend in what troops he might have at One Eye, and that he would ſupply their place with ſome from colonel Caldwell's detachments in Mile Gully. This I communicated to colonel Peart; but he had none there, and the want of proviſions made me leſs anxious to preſs the buſineſs, as I have never been able to get above one day's ſupplies at the poſt at any time ſince I took the command here. Many days we have been entirely out of bread-kind, ſome- times out of beef, and frequently, indeed oftener than otherwiſe, at ſhort allowance of bread-kind, and that frequently of the worſt kind; and if I had not got flour, ſalt beef, and biſcuit from Vere, I do not think I could have maintained the poſt till this time. The officers have, at great expence and in- convenience, almoſt wholly ſupplied their table

from

from thence. I think that the commiffioners muft be very dilatory, otherwife we would have been better fupplied; all that I write to them has no effect. In confequence of its being ftrongly fup-pofed that the remaining maroons and runaways would make for thefe woods, I wrote to colonel Caldwell, in cafe I fhould be obliged to advance further into the woods, that it would be neceffary for me to call on him for part of his detachments to affift me, as I conceived I had too few troops for that bufinefs, and protecting the provifions and am-munition that it would be neceffary to have depo-fited here; at fame time apprized him of the diffi-culty of providing fupplies of provifion, fo that he might judge for himfelf in the propriety of coming forward. His anfwer to me was, that he had in-clofed my letter to general Campbell, and that he did not think he could well leave Mile Gully un-protected; and that, more efpecially, he thought it would be improper to move forward without fur-ther orders, when he confidered the difficulty of procuring provifions. To this I readily affent, and indeed only wifhed for further reinforcement in cafe of actual neceflity, and thought it beft to apprize him of what I thought might be required. You may reft affured there fhall be nothing wanting on my part to defend the poft.

' I have the honour to be, with great refpect, fir, your very humble fervant,   A. Schaw,

   ' Hector's River, January 30th, 1796.

' Hon. major-general Walpole.'

        No. 2.

No. 2

Sir,

' It is my intention to move about 150 or 160 of the maroon prifoners from Montego Bay to the barracks at St. Ann's, where they are to remain.

' You will therefore have every thing prepared for their reception ; and I beg you will notify this to the commiffioners, that they may take the necef-faiy arrangements as to feeding them, &c. &c.

' I have the honour to be your moft obedient humble fervant,   BALCARRES.'

' *Dromilly, February* 2, 1796.
' *Colonel Stevenfon, or officer commanding at St. Ann's.*'

' I fhall write you foon as to the manner of guard-ing them.'

No. 3.

Dear sir,

' I received your letter of February 2d, laft even-ing.

' My objeft has been to keep myfelf free and un-committed; by no means to cramp you in any point that I am not forced to. The maroons are fecured, and in fuch a manner as will leave to the legiflature the full exercife of their powers, when they meet on March 1ft. I do not know your opi-nion refpeƈting the treaty, nor do I defire to know it: I have formed my own, and muft declare it, when I am called upon. You will of courfe take

F   every

every means in your power to get in, or deftroy, the rebels who are ftill out. But what I have anxioufly wifhed for, namely, the fecuring of the perfons of thefe maroons, has been executed, and I can now report with correctnefs and fecurity: While thefe people remained in the Old Town, I could advance nothing but with incorrectnefs and infecurity. As the principle I worked upon is eftablifhed, I cannot poffibly think of troubling you with any detail of mine. You will give what orders you pleafe refpecting the 83d, at Montego-Bay: I gave orders to affemble a proper number of militia, to take the guards. You may always keep any three maroon men with you that you fix upon (Montague James and old Jarrett excepted); but no terms can be held to the rebels now out, that can imprefs an idea that either the country, or myfelf, is bound at all, either by the fpirit of the treaty or the letter of it.

' I mean to divide the maroons, and to fend 160 from Montego-Bay to St. Ann's. I have defired that the maroons themfelves may arrange the families who are to go, and thofe who are to remain; of courfe you will give fuch inftructions on that head as to you feems beft. The 160 will march on Monday next, and I fhall arrange their route. I find I muft neceffarily take fifty of the St. Ann's militia from the pofts in this neighbourhood, to do the duty at St. Ann's.

' The reinforcement fhall be fent down at the
earlieft

earlieft poffible moment; when, I truft, the militia
may be fent home.

      'I am, &c.   BALCARRES.'

                        3d February, 1796.'

'*Hon. major-general Walpole.*'

No. 4.

Old Maroon Town, February 12, 1796.

'MY LORD,

I have the fatisfaction to inform your lordfhip,
that fix maroons, capable of bearing arms, have
this day been brought in by Johnftone, with a
number of women and children. It feems that the
remnant of their body, after the furrender of Johnftone, were met by a maroon of the name of Heath,
who alarmed them by a falfe report of the approach
of the dogs; upon which they fled deep into the
woods, in the direction of Oliphant's, near Hector's
River, as a drum was heard by the party which I
fent from hence, at fome diftance. It is imagined
by Johnftone, and alfo concurs with what I have been
able to gather from the maroons themfelves, that
they are fcattered in different bodies, as they did not
fee fome of thofe whom they expected. Among
thofe who are come in, are two of Holman Harding's
fons: This is their mode; thefe two young men
will reconnoitre us for two or three days, and then
one of them will afk leave to go and bring in his
father and family, and, according to the treatment,
the family will come back and remain. Your

              F 2   lordfhip

lordfhip will be perhaps furprifed to learn, that
fpies from thofe in the woods have more than once
come out, by a circuitous route, to the hills over
the town, and obferved what has been paffing;
they have feen the different bodies, particularly the
laft, fent off to Montego-Bay, and have conftrued
it into treachery on our part. I am told that fome
came to furrender, and upon this went back to the
woods.

' Their want of water is, I underftand, extreme;
they cannot get any but what they draw from the
wild pines; and that, Johnftone tells me, is at this
time very unwholefome. They have a plan, if
driven from thefe woods, of going towards Cave-
River, at a place called Old Woman's Savanna.
As faft as they exhauft the pines at one place, they
move further on.

I have offered no terms but lives; and it may
be neceffary to explain to your lordfhip, that I was
obliged to alter my original plan of attending, with
a detachment of the king's troops, the maroon
party. The want of water, after the firft day's
march, was an infuperable difficulty; and on being
fatisfied in my own mind of the fidelity of the party,
I permitted them to go; and my confidence has
not been forfeited: They were abfent fix days;
and if I had allowed them a longer term, perhaps
more might have been brought in.

' As your lordfhip may perhaps wifh to lay before the legiflature the names of thofe who have
acted with fuch fidelity to the public caufe, I have

to

to mention the names of *Johnstone*, *Smith*, *Sam. James*, *Senior*, *Reid*, *Sam. Barnett*.

' I have the honour to be your lordship's most faithful and obedient servant,

' G. WALPOLE.

' I think it probable, that many of those said to be still in the woods have been killed in the different actions.'

No. 5.

Montego-Bay, 7th February, 1796.

' DEAR SIR,

' In consequence of the orders I received yesterday, I prepared one hundred of the militia to be ready for an escort to the maroons, on Monday morning. I think it right to inform you, that Mr. Werge has just now reported to me his having mentioned to the maroons the orders for separating them, and that they are very much alarmed and discontented, saying they had rather be killed at once.

' I shall, however, be prepared to execute my orders; but wish to have your sentiments on this business in the course of the day.

' As Mr. Werge did not mention the orders for the maroons march until this morning, it is impossible for him to send a return of those that are to go.

' Shaw says, that if the runaways come to the

F 3 knowledge

knowledge of what is to happen, he cannot be anfwerable for them, that they will attempt an
efcape.

‘ Dear fir, your moft humble fervant,

J. Rob. James.’

‘ *Hon. major-general Walpole, Old Maroon Town.*’

No. 6.

‘ My lord,   *February 1ft*, 1796.

‘ To-morrow I intend going into the woods,
with five or fix maroons, and about one hundred
regulars; in all probability we fhall be abfent a
week. I fhall take rockets with me, in order,
fhould we find thofe now out, to call up the dogs,
if they perfift in not furrendering.

‘ It feems that there is a good deal of water in
the Black Grounds, and provifions, feveral fettlements being forming there; and of courfe many
people, whites and negroes, muft be acquainted
with the fpot: The proprietor of Mahogany-Hall
would, I think, not be an improper perfon for
your lordfhip to talk with on the fubject. What
I fhould propofe would be, to fend fome confidential negroes, under the promife of reward, to fearch
for tracks about the places where water and provifions are.

‘ I have the honour to be your lordfhip’s moft
faithful and obedient,

‘ *Earl Balcarres, &c. &c. &c.*   G. Walpole.’

No.

No. 7.

'My dear lord, *February* 11*th*, 1796.

'To-morrow or next day I will fend you a more particular account; but in cafe that you fhould have any arrangements to make as to the packet, I can inform you, that about thirty maroons, including women and children as well as men, will be here, I truft, to-morrow. Smith has arrived with nineteen; Johnftone, who has behaved with great fidelity in this inftance, I expect to-morrow, with the remainder. I am preparing to move the 13th dragoons through the cockpits, from One-Eye. Parkinfon and Palmer are not of the number abovementioned: It feems that the fteps relative to their various removals have reached them; and, confequently, whatever has been done againft their confent much exaggerated. I have all along been afraid of this.

'I fhall fend the maroons to the Bay in two or three days.

'I am your lordfhip's moft obedient,

'G. Walpole.

No. 8.

'My Lord, 18*th February*, 1796.

I omitted in my laft to inform you, that it was my intention to attempt to cut a road to Pond-River, the place where the maroons made their laft ftand, in order that I might avail myfelf of the

water

water at that place, should it become advisable to make any expedition hereafter into the woods in search of the rebels still out; it being perfectly clear, that such a thing must be utterly impracticable from our present posts. I hope, by the direction which we have given to the intended road, that the distance will be shortened from seven to four miles. The maroons arrived at St. Ann's very well satisfied, as colonel Bell informs me. The runaways (for they were so blended as not to be distinguished) were much alarmed : I am told, that there are some among them who have been missing from the estates for years.

' I have the satisfaction to acquaint your lordship, that Mr. Gubbins, of the 13th light dragoons, has entered the woods from the side of St. Elizabeth, at One-Eye: He merits great applause for his perseverance. The commissioners either could not or would not furnish provisions; indeed, I trust that they were not able : The troops undertook, sooner than be debarred their share of enterprize, to cure it themselves: It is curiously done, I make no doubt ; but, such as it is, they have entered the woods, with a resolution to penetrate either directly through the cockpits, or up the banks of Hector's River. The Spaniards are with Mr. Gubbins, and a detachment of Accompong maroons: The whole town shewed great readiness ; but only a few selected as track-men, or rather to give the direction.

' I have

' I have the honour to be your lordfhip's moft faithful and obedient,

' *Earl Balcarres, &c. &c. &c.*   G. WALPOLE.'

' Mr. Robertfon, of the St. Elizabeth's militia, accompanies the expedition.

' I inclofe your lordfhip a lift, the *laft batch* are not included.'

No. 9.

' DEAR SIR,

' From the ftate of the maroon war, I am con‑vinced the country will be of opinion that martial law ought not to be continued :

' That the regular troops, with the affiftance of the black fhot, the Spaniards, &c. are fufficient, as a force to watch over the embers of the rebel‑lion :

And that a party aft may be made of fuch energy as may fuit the purpofe.

' This party bill was in confiderable forward‑nefs at the moment of the late adjournment of the houfe of affembly.

' It is only upon my giving an affurance, that martial law will be taken off as foon as the party aft fhall pafs, that I can hope to carry the queftion, at the next council of war, of continuing martial law.

' Under thefe circumftances, we muft look for‑ward to the application of the regular forces, when the militia go to their homes.

' I think it will take a confiderable force to guard the maroon prifoners. The 17th light dragoons

and

and the 62d regiment may occupy Montego-Bay, Falmouth, and St. Ann's.

' The 17th are to hold themselves in readiness to embark for St. Domingo, when they send shipping to receive them; of which no requisition is as yet made.

' The 83d regiment may occupy the Maroon Town.

' I should be glad to know your wish as to the quartering the 13th light dragoons, on their arrival.

' The 14th regiment of light dragoons are not to remain in this country, if quiet is restored. If, however, the banditti of runaway slaves have gone down to Old Woman's Savanna, they must occupy posts in that neighbourhood; the country that lies behind it I believe never was explored.

' I beg that you will order a list to be taken of all tools and implements, and also what belongs to the hospital, such as cradles.

' Should fresh disturbances break out, we must meet them anew; but there is no alternative at present, but the militia going home, and the furnishing of the guards over the maroons to be done by the regular troops.

' These are my present sentiments; if you wish for any particular disposition of the troops, be so good as to let me know.

' The moment the party act shall pass, I shall
give

give you notice of it, and the militia will begin to move.

‘ I am, &c. &c.   BALCARRES.’

February 20th, 1796.’

‘ *Honourable major-general Walpole.’*

No. 10,

‘ DEAR SIR,

‘ I have heard that fome maroons have been permitted to go from Montego-Bay to Falmouth (to the great offen   of the country) unguarded. I wifh you would fend immediately a ftrong party of regular troops, to relieve the militia in the duty of guarding thefe prifoners. I think the detachment of the 17th light dragoons would do this duty properly; and they will be then ready to embark.

‘ I requeft that you will give them the ftrifteft orders to keep the ftrifteft guard over them; and that this detachment is to be refponfible that no efcape fhall be attempted; for which purpofe each centinel is to have his piece loaded.

‘ You will no doubt take effeftual means to fecure all arms and ammunition, by fending it back, or fecuring it at the Old Town.

‘ Yours, &c.   BALCARRES.’

‘ *King’s houfe, February 29th, 1796.*

‘ *Honourable major-general Walpole.’*

No. 11,

‘ SIR,

‘ It was found neceffary in Weftmorland, at the beginning of the Trelawny maroon rebellion, to

fecure

fecure the perfons of all thefe maroons who refided in Weftmorland.

' As this is a meafure which the fafety of the country required, and it appearing that nearly the whole of thefe maroons, fo refiding in Weftmorland, had no connection with the rebel town, there can be no reafon for keeping thefe people in confinement; they may therefore be enlarged and permitted to return to their homes.

' I have the honour to be your moft obedient humble fervant, BALCARRES.'

' King's houfe, 25th February, 1796.

' Colonel Lawrence, Weftmorland.'

No. 12.

SIR,

' This country is extremely alarmed at the circumftance of feveral of the maroon prifoners having been feen at St. Ann's, going at large without guards. I beg that no relaxation may take place, refpecting guarding againft all poffible efcape of any of thefe maroons.

' I have the honour to be, fir, your moft obedient humble fervant, BALCARRES.'

' King's houfe, March 4th, 1796.

' Colonel Rofe, or officer commanding at St. Ann's Bay.'

No. 13.

Old Maroon Town, March 4th, 1796.

' MY DEAR LORD,

' I arrived here but this day, having ftopped
6   yefterday

yefterday to reft myfelf. I have only to fay that
your lordfhip's orders, as contained in your different difpatches, fhall be executed without delay.
The 17th fhall march the day after to-morrow,
for Montego Bay. I am forry to learn what has
happened; but I hope it has been miftated to your
lordfhip, as I know not of any maroon, except
Smith's family, that have paffed that way; and as
I was here for fome days after, without hearing
any complaint in my correfpondence with colonel
Bell, but the contrary, I fhall truft that the repre-
fentation is not what your lordfhip apprehends to
be the cafe. I have been obliged to bring my
own letter from St. Elizabeth, there being no conveyance from thence to town direct, except on
pofts-days.

' I have the honour to be your lordfhip's moft
faithful and obedient,   G. WALPOLE.'

' I underftand that thofe maroons now out have
faid, that they do not ever mean to do any mifchief;
this we fhall fee.'

No. 14.

' SIR,   <i>King's houfe, 4th March,</i> 1796.

' Every perfon here is alarmed in the higheft
degree, as they underftand that fome of the maroon
prifoners, under your charge, have been feen near
Falmouth, even without a guard.

' I muft entreat that you do give immediately
the ftricteft orders, as to the thoroughly guarding
thefe prifoners; and I truft you will confider the
weight

weight of refponfibility that unqueftionably lies upon yourfelf alone; *that fuch guards and centinels be placed as to prevent the poffibility of any of them effecting their efcape.*

'Yours,   BALCARRES.'
' *Major-general Palmer.*'

No. 15.

' MY DEAR LORD, *March 5th,* 1796.

' The inclofed I fend with all fpeed to your lordfhip; and give you joy of having again the opportunity of finally and effectually terminating the rebellion.

' The letter is written in fo much hurry as not to admit of giving any detail; but the affair I believe to be this : That the maroons, finding that we could get at them, fent forward Shawe, whilft the others were conveying, as well as they could, their families from the dogs. Nothing but the ex-haufted ftate of both the detachment and dogs would have *prevailed*, I am confident, on either the Spaniards or the 13th, to have continued the pur-fuit ; but I fear there was no conquering the want of water ; for nearly three days, I was a witnefs to it ; and my reafons, under thofe circumftances, for permitting the detachment to go forward, your lordfhip is already in poffeffion of.

I fhall grant lives only. I have been too fcanda-loufly traduced already, to exert my judgment for the public good, notwithftanding your lordfhip's
ratification

ratification of the terms heretofore granted. I fhall endeavour to keep the matter afloat till I may be honoured with your lordfhip's commands; for I cannot but apprehend that they may make fome effort to get to windward, defperate as it may appear, fhould they be dealt with too rigidly in their conceptions.

'I hope that the country will not lofe the opportunity.

'I have the honour to be your lordfhip's moft faithful and obedient,   G. WALPOLE.'

'DEAR SIR,

'In your letter of the 5th inftant, you write me that you have been too fcandaloufly traduced already, to exert your judgment for the public good, notwithftanding my ratification of the terms heretofore granted.

'This I do know, that all public men every where will be traduced by reftlefs and violent characters; but my ratifying the treaty which you figned fufficiently marks the fupport which I gave to that meafure; and the refpectable council that advifed me to ratify it, bears you out as well as myfelf. The fame council expreffed themfelves in clear terms, as to the affurance you gave the maroons, that they fhould not be fent off the ifland; and it ftands on the minutes taken at that council, That, provided the maroons performed the 1ft and 3d articles of the treaty, that the fecret articles fhould be complied with.

'Every

‘ Every man, however, will form his own opinion as to thofe two points: Firſt, Whether or not the treaty is a wife one ; Secondly, If it has been per‑ formed. It now lies before the affembly, as well as our correfpondence upon it, from the period of colonel Hull's aftion to the moment of the maroons coming in, inclufive, and alfo my letter dated 2d of February.

‘ In regard to the third article of the treaty, it ſtands upon a matter of faft, to eſtablifh, whether the runaways were furrendered, agreeable to that article or not.

‘ As to the firſt and fecond articles, my mind is made up upon the fubjeft; and my opinion is, that if force had not been fent out againſt them, in con‑ formity to my orders of the 14th of January, iffued in confequence of my receiving your letter of that date, they would not have come in at all.

‘ But from the high fituation which you have filled, from the intercourfe and converfations you have had with thefe maroons, and, above all, that thefe unhappy people may have every circumftance adduced to the affembly that can operate in their favour, it may be fair and right in you to give an opinion, if you are fo inclined, how far, in your conception, thefe people have complied with the articles of that treaty.

‘ I am perfeftly aware, and ſhall hold in my recollеftion, the favourable opinion you have of the Smiths and Johnſtone ; and I ſhall reprefent it to the affembly at a proper time. Whatever opinions
we

we may hold refpecting the treaty, we are united in the fentiment of bringing the bufinefs before the public in the fulleft and faireft manner; and if the ftate of the war can permit of your abfence, I could wifh you here, that we might do it in con‑junction.

' I wifh to make a remark upon the firft part of your letter of the 5th, which runs in thefe words : " I give you joy of having again the opportunity of finally and effectually terminating the rebel‑lion."

' This, I prefume, alludes to the circumftance of your wifhing to keep the maroon prifoners at the Maroon Town, inftead of fending them to the coaft. I really cannot ftate this to have been a difference of opinion between yourfelf and me ; and I am free to confefs that their remaining in that fituation might have been an inducement for thofe ftill out to have come in. But I thought it was playing too deep a game; and if the maroons had given us the flip, I fhould have had a dreadful reckoning to account for to the king, this country, and my own tranquil‑lity of mind.

' I am, &c. &c.   BALCARRES.'
' *March 9th*, 1796.
Honourable major-general Walpole.'

No. 16.

' MY DEAR LORD,   *March 11th*, 1796.
' I have this moment yours of (I think it is) the 9th of March.

G   ' I fend

' I fend you a private letter; make what ufe of it you pleafe. I have no objection to its being fhewn and canvaffed; indeed, I fear that you have been in fome points deceived. The maroons would make out a ftronger cafe, from what paffes by my ear very often, than is imagined. Many of them fay, that the rebellion of—60 would not have been quelled but for them; there are fome of them here who were wounded in that event: Indeed, my dear lord, had there been fuch a body at St. Domingo, the brigands never would have rifen. This may look like being an advocate; but it is my honeft opinion. If Palmer and Parkinfon fhould refufe the terms, which I think they will, you never will conquer them. I fhall offer the terms, and there leave the matter.

' I will not, nor fhall any thing induce me, avail myfelf of that reliance which I fee they have in me, until I am certain that no deceit is intended. I will not be acceffary to fo foul a crime.

' Could not a company of rangers be formed from them, agreeable to the hints which I once laid before you, and the reft difperfed about as free citizens, like the people of colour.

' Johnftone fet out this morning, with D. Shaw, T. Harding, and Bucknor. I do not expect them back till the 19th.

' Content yourfelf, my lord, with this reflection: That the ifland, by firmnefs and humanity together, has been faved, without *a fingle cane deftroyed*; and

at

at a time when the *flaves were fet agog by Mr. Wilberforce.*

' I have the honour to be, in hafte, your lordfhip's moft faithful and obedient,

' G. WALPOLE.'

' One word as to the freedom allowed the maroons; Montego-Bay barrack is not fecure; it is beft
therefore not to feem to miftruft them.'

[*Private*]   *March* 11th, 1796.

' MY DEAR LORD,

' I muft trouble your lordfhip with a few words
in privacy and confidence.

' For fome days paft, I have been in a ftate of
confiderable uneafinefs at a report, which feems to
gain ground, that the legiflature mean to infringe the
capitulation accepted by me and ratified by your
lordfhip.

' My lord, to be plain with you, it was through
my means alone that the maroons were induced to
furrender, from a reliance which they had in my
word, from a conviction impreffed upon them by
me that the white people would never break their
faith.

' All thefe things ftrongly call upon me, as the
inftrumental agent in this bufinefs, to fee a due ob-
fervance of the terms, or, in cafe of violation, to
refign my command; and if that fhould not be
accepted, to declare the facts to the world, and to
leave them to judge how far I ought or ought not to
be implicated in the guilt and infamy of fuch a proceeding. So much the more ftrong is this call upon

G 2   me,

me, as there was no occafion to ratify the terms;
for your lordfhip will well recollect, that I told you
at Caftle-Wemyfs, that the time appointed by me
for fulfilling them was expired, and the terms
therefore null and void; but your lordfhip then
thought, that there was fo much of advantage to the
country in thofe terms, that it would be beft not to
give them up.

' As the great object of the war is now declared
to be accomplifhed, I fhall fhortly folicit your lordfhip for permiffion to return to England, with an
intention to retire from the fervice.

' I am your lordfhip's moft faithful and obedient,   G. WALPOLE.'

' Earl Balcarres, &c. &c. &c.'

' DEAR SIR,

' I am honoured by both your letters of March
11th. If I had not looked upon the treaty figned by
you as advantageous to the country, under the exift-
ing circumftances, I never would have ratified it: But
the country has a right to every advantage which
that treaty affords it and I am decidedly of opinion, that if the terms of the treaty have been
complied with by the maroons, that the country is
bound in honour not to fend them off the ifland.
So far I go with you, and fo far I will fupport you;
but, I fhall certainly leave it with the legiflature to
decide, whether that treaty has been obferved, or
not: Indeed, they will decide that for themfelves,
as a matter of right inherent in them.

6   ' All

All I can say is, that I have not the smallest light upon what their decision will be; but I assure you, those strong sentiments which you have expressed relative to those maroons shall fairly be canvassed. I do not enter into what the country in its wisdom ought to do. I feel we have done our duty as soldiers: The executive power, in my person, has amply supported you, by ratifying the treaty which you acceded to.

' But, in a political consideration of this subject, the country will not be guided either by your politics or mine. There is a word in your last letters, namely, *capitulation*, is used instead of *treaty*: It has always hitherto been mentioned as a treaty; perhaps it may be a distinction without a difference. Be it what it may, I look upon my responsibility to the public as *equally* committed; for surely, if there is any thing upon earth in which a legislature has a right to exercise its judgment, *it is internal rebellion.* Under the whole circumstances of the case, you have done extremely right in with-holding any offer to the rebel maroons still out, excepting *lives, and their being placed exactly in the same situation, and to share the fate, whatever it may be, of the maroon prisoners now in our possession.* I cannot offer them more, until the sentiments of the legislature respecting those now in should be communicated to me.

' In respect to your going home, I shall be extremely happy in doing whatever may be agreeable to yourself in this point: But I regret your deter-

mination

mination of quitting the fervice, in which you are
fo well advanced.

'I have the honour to remain, very fincerely,
yours,   BALCARRES.'
                    'King's houfe, 16 March, 1796.
'Hon. major-general Walpole.'

No. 17.

'MY LORD,   March 13th, 1796.

'I have this moment the honour of your lordfhip's difpatches of the 10th, one number 2, the
other not of any number, but inclofing a meffage
from the affembly.

'I apprehend a variety of opinion may arife
upon the third article: A vaft number, I believe,
of runaways are out; but Johnftone and Smith
have frequently affured me, that, the maroons once
in, no difficulty would arife as to the others. I
underftand that David Shaw has mentioned, that,
as a preparatory ftep towards fecuring the runaways, they have taken the fire-arms from them.
By the way, the fecond article implies the whole of
the fecret article.

'Your lordfhip has, I well know, been of opinion, that the force fent out on the 14th induced
the maroons to come in. I think not; and my
opinion is grounded on this fact, that I met the maroons, about half a mile from the advanced poft,
coming in with loads on their backs of clothes and
children. They muft therefore have moved more
                                                than

than half way the day before; and certainly no one
knew of my motions here. A maroon of the name
of Heath turned on hearing the dogs, and went to
Palmer and Parkinſon, and told them that a *trap
was laid*, and the dogs ſent round in a different direction. Johnſtone came up to me, ſome time after
in the day, and informed, that this had been juſt
told him; adding, that if I had left him to his own
direction, he would have remained till he had ſeen
every one of them out, but that he came before, having heard (which was true enough) that
I had ſaid, that if he came the reſt would come
too.

'The wiſdom of the treaty cannot be much
doubted, as treble the number of troops would not
have brought in ſo many maroons in twelve months
more. Your lordſhip will permit me to obſerve,
that the opinions of the field-officers on the ſpot
have never differed.

'It was not ſo much the ſending the maroons
from hence, as the time of doing it, that I with-
ſtood. I wiſhed to have had the opportunity to
have been taken when I might ſee it beſt. The
laſt party I was very averſe to ſending away; it
conſiſted of 24 men, compoſed in a great meaſure
of the families of Smith and Johnſtone. Johnſtone was deſirous to ſtay, he ſaid, with me; and I
had aſſured him of ſo much being done; and I well
knew what effect the ſending him away under a
guard would have, if perceived from the hills. I
have to thank your lordſhip for your great attention

to

to me, and giving yourself so much trouble to explain your sentiments to me: I only aim at an honest discharge of my duty. I am anxious to keep my faith with those maroons now surrendered. Sure I am, that Jamaica has been saved by the terms of surrender, and that the not adhering to them may be productive, one day or other, of the loss of the colony.

' I have the honour to be with all deference, your lordship's most faithful and obedient,

' G. Walpole.

' If your lordship wishes for my attendance in Spanish-Town, I shall set out, if nothing material occurs, on the 19th or 20th.

' Should your lordship not find my attendance necessary, you will have the goodness to let me know of it.

No. 18.

' Sir,   St. Ann, March 14th, 1796.

' A detachment of the 62d regiment, consisting of one captain, three serjeants, and forty-nine rank and file, arrived here at eight o'clock yesterday morning; and, in obedience to the governor's orders which came to my hands (as the commanding officer at St. Ann) I delivered the maroon prisoners and runaways, at five o clock yesterday afternoon, to captain Daly, who commanded the detachment, and took his receipt for them; a copy of which is at foot.

' I have dismissed the militia until further orders, agreeable to his lordship's directions.

' I have

' I have the honour to be, fir, your obedient fervant,   T. JENKINS, *lt. col. St. Ann's reg.'*

" Received, March 13th, 1796, as prifoners in the St. Ann's barrack, from lieut. col. Jenkins, one hundred and fixty maroons (in which are included the runaways), all in good health, excepting two perfons named Sukey and Lawfon.

(Signed)   " HYATH. RD. DALY, *capt. 62d. Col. Rofe, Southfield.'*

No. 19.

' DEAR SIR,

' The Iris muft take on board the maroon
men at Falmouth, fay	2Q
62d regt. troops to guard them	9
The Iris muft then drop down to Montego-Bay, and take on board the maroon men, about	51
Boys, ditto	54
62d regt. the troops about	75
Total	**209**

Exclufive of the officers, &c.

The Thomas muft go to St. Ann's, and take
on board maroon men, about	16
Maroon boys, ditto	12
Runaways, ditto	46
Boys, ditto	16
Troops, 62d regt. ditto	54
	144

The

‘ The other veffels are the Mercury, the Barbara, and the Conqueft; which three veffels will take all the women and children. It may be in your power perhaps to make one of thefe three veffels work up to St. Ann's, if fhe can work to windward better than the Thomas, and there receive the troops and maroons, which fhe can deliver on board the Thomas at fea.

‘ It is not eafy to give orders fufficiently pofitive and precife to reach the different circumftances attending this embarkation; and the more fo, as the three privateer veffels, or fome of them, may be cruifing; but Mr. Gillies will give you every information. The veffels allotted for this fervice are, the Mercury, Conqueft, Barbara, Iris, and Thomas, in which all the maroons, the runaways, and 62d regiment, are to be embarked, and to proceed to Port-Royal. Should you not have it in your power to fend all, by reafon of the cruifers not being got at, you will fend all the males in preference to the females, and the cruifers will take the women whenever there is an opportunity of giving them orders to receive thefe women on board.

‘ Thefe veffels muft be victualled proper for the fervice they are going upon. The whole. ought to collect, and fail together.

‘ You are now in poffeffion of the outlines of my fentiments; and, that you may perform this very effential fervice to your country, I muft entreat that you will be fo good as to accept of being fole

fole commiffioner for the embarkation and failing of
thofe people.

‘ I fend you a commiffion accordingly ; and believe me to be, &c &c. &c.

‘ BALCARRES,’

‘ King's houfe, March 16th, 1796.

‘ Perhaps you had as well let the Iris go down
before you declare your powers, or our intentions.

‘ James Galloway, efquire, Falmouth.’

‘ By his honour the right honourable ALEXANDER
earl of BALCARRES, lieutenant-governor and
commander in chief of his majefty's ifland of
Jamaica, &c. &c. &c.

‘ Whereas I have thought fit to appoint James
Galloway, efquire, to be the fole commiffioner for
the purpofe of embarking all the maroons and 6 2d
regiment on board the veffels Iris, Thomas, Mercury, Conqueft, and Barbara :

‘ I hereby require and order all officers having
the charge of thefe maroons to caufe them to be
embarked, at the requifition of the faid commiffioner James Galloway, efquire.

‘ I direct the different detachments of the 62d
regiment, now doing duty over the maroons, to
embark according to the allotment of the faid commiffioner to each veffel, and on the day which he
fhall name :

‘ That

' That the several detachments of the 62d regiment are responsible for the safe delivery of those maroons to captain Dobbin, of Fort-Augusta.

' That all the commissioners for the several parishes are required to be aiding and assisting for the due victualling, &c. of the vessels; and I hereby authorize the said commissioner James Galloway, esquire, to give what orders he thinks best suited to the nature of the service, to the five captains of the five above-mentioned vessels, and especially that he may name one of them to command the whole; who will report on his arrival at Port-Royal, both to the officer commanding the royal navy and also to captain Bingham of his majesty's ship Jamaica.

' I do hereby appoint the said James Galloway, esquire, to be the sole commissioner for the above purposes.

' *Given under my hand and seal at arms, at St.* *Jago de la Vega, the* 16th *day of March,* *Annoque Domini,* 1796.   BALCARRES.

No. 20.

My lord,   *March* 17th, 1796.

' Four maroons, dispatched by Johnstone, arrived yesterday, with a message to inform me, that he was on his way to me with the *whole remaining body* of the maroons, and, if I am not misinformed, of the runaways also. Whether this is to surrender, or whether it is meant *first* to be a conference, I cannot ascertain till they arrive.

' Your lordship will no doubt view the conduct of Johnstone, in this latter business particularly, in a very meritorious light. The names of those who

accompanied

accompanied him and affifted on the expedition are
as *per* margin.

' I have the honour to be your lordfhip's moft
faithful fervant,

' *T. Harding,*   G. WALPOLE.'
' *Bucknor,*
' *D. Shaw.*'

No. 21.

' MY DEAR LORD,   *March* 21*ft*, 1796.

' I cannot be with you fo foon as I could wifh.
The maroons now in the woods are thirteen in number: I have expected them yefterday and this day.
It feems that thefe were out hunting wild hog s; and
Johnftone, eager to bring out as many as he could,
would not wait, but left fome of the women to tell
thefe, at their return, what had happened.

' Parkinfon fays, that I may rely on their furrender ; and fo fure is he of it, that he left his wife and
children behind him. He defired to fend in two of
his party, but did not wifh to go himfelf. As foon as
the whole arrive, I fhall fend them down to Montego-Bay under the non-commiffioned officer of
the 16th, and ten men of the 17th dragoons, whom
I was obliged to detain here. The 11th may as well
remain at Montego-Bay till their embarkation for
Europe.

' The maroons I perceive coming in at this inftant. The fire-arms brought in by *Parkinfon's*
party are *forty-four.* The number of *maroons, thirty-
fix bearing arms.*

Mr.

Mr. Gallimore's fufee I fhall return to his friends, at their requeft.

‘ I hope to leave this place on Thurfday for Spanifh-Town.

‘ I thank your lordfhip for acceding to my wifhes refpecting my going home; and fhall prepare to go by the next fleet: As to my remaining in the army, the candidates who ftand before me are too numerous to allow me any very fanguine hopes of preferment.

‘ I have not fpoken to Skinner on the matter; but if he went home with your lordfhip's difpatches, it might perhaps fecure his local rank to him in Europe; but that may be done otherwife : Although he has not been actually engaged, he has been of the moft material fervice. I fee very clearly, that when it comes to hard work, he is an officer to be depended upon.

‘ I have the honour to be your lordfhip's moft faithful and obedient,

‘ G. Walpole.’

‘ I could wifh your lordfhip would obtain permiffion for Charles Samuels, a maroon, brother to Smith, to remain with me.

‘ Bowen Harding cannot be removed, on account of his wound; and I fhall allow his brother to remain here with him.

G. W.’

No. 22.

No. 22.

'My lord,   *Falmouth*, 22*d March*, 1796.

'I had the honour of your lordship's letter of 16th instant, with the commission and instructions relative to the maroons.

'I take the liberty of assuring your lordship, that no exertion shall be wanting on my part, to complete that service according to your lordship's wish.

'Mr. Quarrell is just arrived here from the Old Maroon Town, and says the whole of the maroons and runaways are come in: This is fortunate; it will enable the whole to be sent round together.

'The Iris and Thomas were seen this morning off Montego Bay, and may be expected here to-morrow.

'I have the honour to be your lordship's very faithful and obedient servant,

JAMES GALLOWAY.'

No. 23.

'My dear lord,   *March* 22*d*, 1796.

'I have this moment received your letters No. 1, 2, and 3.

'As affairs are now so much altered, I think that I may as well go to Spanish Town: Indeed, should I defer it, and the journey hereafter be necessary, I may then be without a conveyance, for my own horses are starved.

'My wish to retire was, in a great degree, connected with a presage which I had of future circumstances

ſtances with regard to the maroons; perhaps thoſe may now be altered. I was fearful leſt it ſhould ſeem that I had drawn the maroons into a treaty which I knew was hereafter to be broken; my re-ſignation was meant to declare my entire ignorance of ſuch an intention; private reaſons might alſo operate in ſome degree, but they would not have prevailed alone.

' I remain your lordſhip's moſt faithful and obe-dient,   G. WALPOLE.'

No. 24.

' MY LORD,   *Falmouth*, 23d *March*, 1796.

' I have juſt received information from Mr. Gil-lies, that brig Conqueſt has not been heard of for theſe ten days; that the Mercury is in Montego Bay, ſhort of hands; the Iris and Thomas have not yet made their appearance. From the addi-tional number of maroons and runaways come in, there will be much deficiency in the ſhipping to carry them round. I therefore take the liberty of ſubmitting to your lordſhip's conſideration the moving of thoſe at St. Ann's by land, unleſs ſome other veſſel could be had for them.

' I have the honour to be your lordſhip's moſt faithful and obedient ſervant, JAMES GALLOWAY.'

THURSDAY, 24*th March*, 1796.

Ordered, That the following meſſage be ſent to the council:

" *May*

" *May it please your honours,*

" We are ordered by the houfe to acquaint you, that there being matters on bufinefs of the utmoft importance to this ifland before the houfe, they defire you will appoint a fpecial fecret committee of your board, to join a fpecial fecret committee of the houfe in a free conference on fuch matters; and, if your honours agree thereto, you will be pleafed to appoint your number, time, and place."

Ordered, That Mr. Redwood and Mr. Wedderburn be a committee to carry the above meffage to the council; who returning, reported the delivery thereof.

A meffage from the council, by their clerk, as follows :

" *Mr. Speaker,*

' I am commanded by the council to acquaint the houfe, in anfwer to their meffage of this day, that they agree to the free conference therein propofed, and have appointed three of their board to be a fpecial fecret committee, to join a fpecial fecret committee of the houfe for that purpofe, on Wednefday next, at twelve o'clock, in the council-chamber."

Ordered, That Mr. Murray, Mr. Wedderburn, Mr. Vaughan, Mr. Redwood, Mr. Cuthbert, Mr. Chief Juftice, Mr. Shirley, Mr. Edwards, and Mr. M'Lean, be a committee to manage the faid free conference.

Ordered, That the clerk of this houfe do attend at the faid free conference, with all fuch papers and documents as may be neceffary.

H   Ordered,

Ordered, That the committee appointed to meet a committee of the council, in a free conference, do lay before the houſe all ſuch evidence or information on which they may ground their report, that has not yet been laid before the houſe.

WEDNESDAY, 20*th* *April,* 1796.

Mr. Murray, from the ſpecial ſecret committee appointed to join a ſpecial ſecret committee of the council, in a free conference on matters of buſineſs of the utmoſt importance to the iſland, reported,

That both committees accordingly met; and his honour the lieutenant-governor's meſſage of the 2d day of March laſt, and the papers therewith ſent, and his honour's meſſage of the 23d March laſt, and the papers therewith ſent, alſo a petition of ſundry perſons known under the denomination of maroons, preſented to the houſe on the 30th day of November laſt, and alſo his honour's meſſage of the 3d day of December laſt, and the petition of the Trelawny maroons then in Kingſton barracks, therewith ſent, were ſeverally read; and alſo an extract of a letter from his grace the duke of Portland to his honour the lieutenant-governor, to the ſaid report reſpectively annexed, having been laid before the joint committee by his honour, the ſame were alſo ſeverally read : And that the joint committee having propoſed certain queſtions in writing to his honour the lieutenant-governor, which queſtions and his honour's anſwers thereto are to the ſaid report annexed,

annexed, the joint committee thereupon came to the following refolutions:

1*ft*. That it is the opinion of the joint committee, that all runaway flaves, who joined the Trelawny maroons in rebellion, ought to be dealt with according to law.

2*d.* That it is the opinion of the joint committee, that all perfons of free condition, who joined the rebels, ought to be dealt with according to law.

3*d.* That it is the opinion of the joint committee, that the thirty-one maroons who furrendered at Vaughansfield, under the proclamation of the 8th of Auguft, together with the fix deputies taken up at St. Ann's, having come in before any actual *hoftilities* commenced, fhould be fent off the ifland, and fome fettlement provided for them in another country.

4*th.* That it is the opinion of the joint committee, that Smith, Dunbar, and Williams, with their wives and children, and the two boys who came in on the 1ft of January, are entitled to the benefit of the treaty.

5*th.* That it is the opinion of the joint committee, that all the maroons who are confined in Kingfton, Falmouth, and elfewhere, that have petitioned the honourable houfe of affembly to be permitted to take the benefit of an act, paffed in the year 1791, intituled " An Act to repeal ' An act for the

better

better order and government of the negroes belonging to the feveral negro towns, and for preventing them from purchafing of flaves; and for
encouraging the faid negroes to go in purfuit of
runaway flaves; and for other purpofes therein
mentioned;' and for giving the maroon negroes
further protection and fecurity; for altering the
mode of trial; and for other purpofes," not having been at any time in rebellion, be allowed to do
fo, according to the prayer of their petition.

6th. That it is the opinion of the joint committee, that the maroons who petitioned his honour
the lieutenant-governor, on the 3d of November
laft (the thirty-one maroons who furrendered at
Vaughansfield excepted) being alfo guiltlefs of any
act of rebellion, be likewife admitted to take the
benefit of the faid act.

7th. That it is the opinion of the joint committee, that all the maroons who furrendered after the
firft of January, and until the 10th day of March
laft (within which period Johnftone and his party
came in), not having complied with the terms of
the treaty, are not entitled to the benefit thereof, and
ought to be fhipped off the ifland; but the joint committee are of opinion, that they ought to be fent to
a country in which they will be free, and fuch as may
be beft calculated, by fituation, to fecure the ifland
againft the danger of their return; that they ought
to be provided with fuitable clothing and neceffaries for the voyage, and maintained at the public
expence

expence of this ifland for a reafonable time after their arrival at the place of their deftination.

8th. That it is the opinion of the joint committee, that Parkinfon and Palmer, and all the maroons who came in with them, are entitled to their lives only, but ought to be fent off the ifland; and as their conduct was marked with aggravated guilt, they ought, in the manner of their being fent off the ifland, to be dealt with more rigoroufly than thofe in the clafs mentioned in the preceding refolution.

9th. That it is the opinion of the joint committee, that as there may be among the rebels a few who, by their repentance, fervices, and good behaviour fince their furrender, may have merited protection and favour, that it be recommended to his honour the lieutenant-governor to permit fuch to remain in the ifland, together with their wives and children; and to diftinguifh them by any other marks of favour, as his honour in his difcretion may think proper.

10th. That it is the opinion of the joint committee, that the lieutenant-governor, in complying with the matters mentioned and recommended in the preceding refolutions, fhould be fully indemnified at the public expence.

Extract of a letter from his grace the duke of Portland to his honour the lieutenant-governor, referred to in the annexed report, dated Whitehall, 8th January, 1796.

' From the cordiality and zeal with which the militia and the inhabitants in general co-operate

with

with your lordſhip, I have no doubt of your being
able to take ſuch meaſures againſt the maroons as
will moſt ſpeedily and effectually tend to their reduction.

'The very defence which, from their local ſituation and other cauſes, they have been able to make
againſt a very ſuperior force, renders it eſſential
that the iſland, in any terms which may be granted
them, ſhould be ſecured againſt the poſſibility of a
ſimilar inſurrection.

'This will, I conceive, be beſt effected, firſt, by
not reſtoring to them their diſtrict; and, ſecondly,
by placing them in ſuch a ſituation within the
iſland (if it cannot be done out of it, which would
be preferable) as will, from its nature, incapaci-
tate them from contriving further miſchief.'

*Queſtions propoſed to his honour the lieutenant-governor,
and his honour's anſwers thereto, referred to in the
annexed report.*

Q. 'Whether general Walpole, upon the ſurrender of Palmer and Parkinſon, and other maroons in their party, had promiſed any thing more
than ſafety of their lives?

A. 'Lives only.'

Q. 'Upon what terms were Harvey and Williams, the two brown men, received, and did they
ſurrender in the character of maroons?'

A. 'They ſurrendered as maroons, without any
ſpecial conditions, and after January 1ſt.'

Q. 'Were the runaways ſurrendered by the
maroons, and were they received upon any expreſs
terms?'

A. 'No

A. ' No runaways have been furrendered by the maroons; they came in in the character of maroons.'

Refolved, That the confideration of the above report be poftponed until Saturday next.

SATURDAY, 23d April, 1796.

Refolved, That the confideration of the report from the fpecial fecret committee appointed to join a fpecial fecret committee of the council, in a free conference on matters of bufinefs of the utmoft importance to this ifland, be further poftponed until Wednefday next.

TUESDAY, 26th April, 1796.

A meffage from the council, by their clerk, as follows:

" *Mr. Speaker,*

" I am commanded by the council to acquaint the houfe, that they have agreed to the report made by the chairman of their fpecial fecret committee appointed to meet a fpecial fecret committee of the houfe, on matters of bufinefs of the utmoft importance to this ifland."

Ordered, That the above meffage do lie on the table, to be perufed by the members.

WEDNESDAY, 27th April, 1796.

The order of the day for the taking into confideration the report from the fpecial fecret committee appointed

H 4

pointed

pointed to join a ſpecial ſecret committee of the council, in a free conference on matters of buſineſs of the utmoſt importance to this iſland, being read;

And the ſaid report being again read;

And a motion being made, that the houſe do agree thereto;

The houſe divided:

The noes went forth:

Ayes, 21 : Mr. Redwood, Mr. Bryan, Mr. Hal-ſted, Mr. Campbell, Mr. Foulks, Mr. Cockburn, Mr. Roſs, Mr. Chief-Juſtice, Mr. Johnſtone, Mr. Taylor, Mr. Thompſon, Mr. Cuthbert, Mr. M'Lean, Mr. Wedderburn, Mr. White, Mr. Vaughan, Mr. Murray, Mr. Chriſtie, Mr. P. Fuller, Mr. Shir-ley, and Mr. Edwards:

Noes, 13 :—Mr. Quarrell, Mr. G. Fuller, Mr. Hodges, Mr. Galbraith, Mr. Fitch, Mr. Mathiſon, M . Woolfrys, Mr. Stewart, Mr. Grant, Mr. An-derſon, Mr. Oſborn, Mr. Henckell, and Mr. Deans:

So it was reſolved in the affirmative.

A motion being made, that the proceedings of the houſe this day, relative to the report from the ſpecial ſecret committee appointed to join a ſpecial ſecret committee of the council, in a free confer-ence on matters of buſineſs of the utmoſt impor-tance to this iſland, be publiſhed in the Royal Ga-zette, St. Jago Gazette, and Cornwall Chronicle, for one month;

A debate thereon ariſing, and the queſtion being put, it paſſed in the negative.

A motion

A motion being made, that a meſſage be ſent to the council, to acquaint their honours, that the houſe had agreed to the report made by the chairman of the ſpecial ſecret committee appointed to join a ſpecial ſecret committee of the council, in a free conference on matters of buſineſs of the utmoſt importance to this iſland;

A debate thereon ariſing, and the queſtion being put, it was reſolved in the affirmative.

Ordered, That the following meſſage be ſent to the council:

" *May it pleaſe your honours,*

" We are ordered by the houſe to acquaint you, that they have agreed to the report made by the chairman of their ſpecial ſecret committee appointed to join a ſpecial ſecret committee of your board, in a free conference on matters of buſineſs of the utmoſt importance to this iſland."

Ordered, That Mr. Murray and Mr. Wedderburn be a committee to carry the above meſſage to the council; who returning, reported the delivery thereof.

THURSDAY, 28*th April,* 1796.

Reſolved, That a clauſe be inſerted in the poll-tax bill for paying to the order of the commiſſioners appointed by law for ſtating and ſettling the public accounts, a ſum or ſums not exceeding 25,000 *l.* in order to carry into effect the reſolutions of the joint committees of the council and
the

the affembly, agreed to by the houfe on the 27th inftant.

Refolved, That a meffage be fent to his honour the lieutenant-governor, with a copy of the above refolution.

FRIDAY, 29*th April*, 1796.

Ordered, That the following meffage be fent to his honour the lieutenant-governor :

" *May it pleafe your honour*,

" We are ordered by the houfe to wait on your honour, and to lay before you a copy of a refolution of the houfe of yefterday."

Ordered, That Mr. Grant and Mr. Campbell be a committee to wait on his honour with the above meffage; who returning, reported the delivery thereof.

Refolved, That the following meffage be fent to his honour the lieutenant-governor :

" *May it pleafe your honour*,

" We are ordered by the   houfe   to lay before your honour their   refolutions refpecting matters of the utmoft importance to this ifland."

Ordered, That the following meffage be fent to the council :

" *May it pleafe your honours*,

" The houfe having agreed on a meffage to his honour the lieutenant-governor, we are ordered to

8   lay

lay the fame before your honours, and to defire your concurrence."

Ordered, That Mr. Murray and Mr. Wedder-burn be a committee to carry the above meffage, and alfo the meffage to his honour the lieutenant-governor, to the council; who returning, reported the delivery thereof.

A meffage from the council, by their clerk, as follows:

" *Mr. Speaker,*

" I am commanded by the council to acquaint the houfe, that they have agreed to the meffage to his honour the lieutenant-governor, fent them this day by the houfe for their concurrence; and that they defire the houfe will be pleafed to fill it up accordingly."

Ordered, That Mr. Murray, Mr. Wedderburn, Mr. Chief-Juftice, Mr. Cuthbert, Mr. Edwards, Mr. Shirley, Mr. M'Lean, Mr. Vaughan, and Mr. Redwood, be a committee to join a committee of the council, to wait on his honour the lieutenant-governor with the meffage agreed to this day.

Ordered, That the following meffage be fent to the council:

" *May it pleafe your honours,*

" We are ordered by the houfe to acquaint you, that they have filled up the blanks with the words " council and," " of affembly," and "joint," in the meffage to his honour the lieutenant-governor, agreeable

able to your honour's meſſage of this day, and have
appointed a committee to join a committee of your
board, to wait on his honour the lieutenant-governor with the ſame."

Ordered, That Mr. M'Lean and Mr. Foulks be
a committee to carry the above meſſage to the
council; who returning, reported the delivery
thereof.

A meſſage from the council, by their clerk, as
follows:

" *Mr. Speaker*,

" I am commanded by the council to acquaint
the houſe, that agreeable to their meſſage of this day,
they have appointed a committee of three of their
board to join a committee of the houſe, to wait on
his honour the lieutenant-governor with the joint
meſſage immediately."

Then the committee went up; and being returned, Mr. Murray, from the committee, reported,
that the joint committee had waited on his honour
the lieutenant-governor with the joint meſſage accordingly,

SUNDAY, 1ſt *May*, 1796.

Ordered, That the following meſſage be ſent to
his honour the lieutenant-governor:

" *May it pleaſe your honour*,

" We are ordered by the houſe to wait on your
honour; and to requeſt that you will be pleaſed to
give

give orders for the difmiffion of the chaffeurs and the dogs, the rebellion being now at an end. We cannot but take this opportunity of expreffing our acknowledgments of the eminent advantages derived by the importation of the chaffeurs and dogs, in compliance with the general wifhes of the ifland: Nothing can be clearer, than that if they had been off the ifland, the rebels could not have been induced to furrender, from their almoft inacceffible faftneffes. We are happy to have it in our power to fay, that terror excited by the appearance of the dogs has been fufficient to produce fo fortunate an event; and we cannot but highly approve that attention to humanity fo ftrongly proved by their being ordered in the rear of the army.

Ordered, That Mr. Ofborn and Mr. Cuthbert be a committee to wait on his honour with the above meffage; who returning, reported the delivery thereof.

(True extracts.)

JAMES LEWIS,
Clerk to the Affembly.

F I N I S.

For EU product safety concerns, contact us at Calle de José Abascal, 56–1°, 28003 Madrid, Spain or eugpsr@cambridge.org.

www.ingramcontent.com/pod-product-compliance
Ingram Content Group UK Ltd.
Pitfield, Milton Keynes, MK11 3LW, UK
UKHW012346130625
459647UK00009B/574